Galen's *Institutio Logica*

GALEN'S
Institutio Logica

English Translation,
Introduction, and Commentary

JOHN SPANGLER KIEFFER

The Johns Hopkins Press · Baltimore

This book has been brought to
publication with the assistance of
a grant from The Ford Foundation.

*To
Roxana*

Preface

For my view of Galen as a scientist and the importance of the *Institutio Logica* for his work, I am indebted to Professor Ludwig Edelstein, whose views expressed in "Recent Trends in the Interpretation of Ancient Science" (*Journal of the History of Ideas*, Vol. XIII, 1952) offer a novel and convincing estimate of the newness of science in Imperial days. In private conversation Dr. Edelstein has kindly amplified these views for me. I am not certain that I have grasped his meaning correctly, so that any misinterpretation of Galen as a scientist is my own and not Dr. Edelstein's. Nevertheless he has provided me with a starting point of interpretation. For this, and other assistance, I am deeply grateful to him.

April, 1964   J. S. K.

Contents

Galen's *Institutio Logica*

Introduction

Galen's short treatise, *An Introduction to Logic*, has interested scholars since its discovery in 1844 as the only textbook of elementary logic surviving from the Ancient Greek world. It is, however, even more interesting when read as a work of Galen's. For it exhibits certain peculiarities which become intelligible in the light of an understanding of what Galen stands for as a scientist, and conversely, these features of the work help us see Galen in a better light than was possible in the recent past. The peculiarities are that the text presents logical doctrines that are known to be Peripatetic, others that are known to be Stoic, and some that are neither; that the presentation of these doctrines is accompanied by a criticism of some of the Peripatetic and Stoic views, so that the author of the work cannot be classified as belonging to either school; that the attitude of the author to logic in general seems to be different from the views both of the early logicians and of the scholastic commentators such as Alexander of Aphrodisias. In short, the work belongs to no traditional philosophical school and yet cannot be called eclectic either, since it exhibits an independence of judgment and a grasp of principle that transcends the usual meaning given to the term eclectic.

What Galen stands for as a scientist has until recently been misunderstood by most historians of ancient thought. In Galen's view science is a unified enterprise, autonomous from philosophy, and dependent for its progress on the co-operative endeavors of generations of scholars. We have abundant evidence in Galen's writings that he found the discordance of views (*diaphônia*) held by the various sects of philosophy and of science to be both shocking and discouraging and that only the fact that all sects agreed that the methods of mathematics produced certain proof kept him from becoming a Pyrrhonian skeptic (*De Libris Propriis*, Kuehn, XIX, 39f). Another text (*De Ordine Librorum*, Kuehn, XIX, 50) adds that most of the adherents of the various sects know no reason why they belong to one rather than another sect.

Out of dissatisfaction with this state of affairs Galen developed his own convictions of what science is. He goes on to declare in the passage just cited that in his book *De Optima Secta* he undertook to show not that the sect bearing the name of this or that philosophy or physician was best, but that only he who had an understanding of scientific demonstration and was without prejudice for or against any sect would, if willing to pursue truth and criticize the opinions of the other sects, be able to discover the best sect.

This leads to the consequence that there is just one science responsible to the discovery of truth and not confined by philosophical dogma. There is not, as the disputes of the sects implied, a Stoic science or a Peripatetic science or any other special sect.   Thus science, because it is a single thing, transcending the sects, is autonomous as well.   This does not mean that science is divorced from philosophy.   Galen's essay, "That the Best Physician is also a Philosopher" (Kuehn, I, 53–63), emphatically asserts the converse.   The autonomy of science means that it is free from having to support a given philosophical position. Lastly, in this same essay Galen asserts the co-operative nature of science and its tendency to progress from generation to generation.   He says:

> The fact that we are born later than the ancients and receive from them the arts in an advanced state, is no small advantage.   At any rate, things that took Hippocrates a long time to discover, one can now learn in a few years and one can employ the rest of his life in the discovery of things that remain to be learned.

A unified, autonomous, co-operative, and progressive enterprise, proceeding by rational methods to demonstrate the truth about things observed in this world, owes much to Aristotle, Theophrastus, and Chrysippus, but most of all it owes them the duty of correcting any errors they may have made and rescuing them from the discord into which the prejudice and even stupidity of their followers had led the schools that bore their names.   Galen's understanding of scientific method is fundamentally derived from Aristotle and Theophrastus, but he has created a fundamentally different science from theirs through his reaction against the *diaphônia* of the schools.   The hints of bad blood between Galen and Alexander have perhaps some reason.*

The *Institutio*, then, may be a work that is absolutely unique, written not from the standpoint of any sect, but from the standpoint of an introduction to the method of science viewed in this new way.   It is, moreover, not a mere schoolbook.   Brief as it is, it contains indications of a man whose life's work has been the transformation of the traditional logic into the method appropriate to a new stage in the history of science.†

---

* For these hints see I. von Mueller, *Ueber Galens Werk vom Wissenschaftlichen Beweis*, p. 22.

† For Galen's position as scientist see L. Edelstein in *Journal of the History of Ideas*, XIII (1952), 602–4.

A number of questions arise concerning the *Institutio* that are pre-
liminary to the considerations outlined in the preceding paragraphs.
There is, first, some question as to Galen's authorship of the work.
Then the contents of the book suggest questions about the state of
knowledge about logic at the time it was written. A further question,
already partially dealt with, is the author's point of view about logic.
Lastly, how much of the work is transcription of previously existing texts,
and how much is in some sense original?

Detailed discussion of most of these points belongs in the commentary
following the translation. It may be useful to the reader to treat all the
questions in a general way in this introduction, in order that he may read
the translation and commentary with a background of understanding.
The gaps in our knowledge are so large that any discussion of the questions
raised must be tentative.

The question of authorship comes first, partly because it may be more
easily disposed of than the others by reference to the work of Karl
Kalbfleisch in demonstrating the authenticity of the work, and partly
because the discussion of the other questions will go differently if we do
not accept Galen as the author.

There is only one known manuscript of the work. It was discovered
in 1844 by Minoidas Mynas in a monastery on Mt. Athos. It is now in
Paris, in the Bibliothèque Nationale, as *Supplementum Graecum, Codex
635*. It is written by the same thirteenth-century scribe who copied
Porphyry's *ad Gaurum*, falsely assigned to Galen. Mynas published an
edition of the *Institutio* in Paris in 1844. The only other edition is that
of Karl Kalbfleisch, in the Teubner Library, Leipzig, 1896, from the
preface of which most of the above information is taken. (For German
translations by Orth and Mau see the bibliography. There has been no
complete English translation.) The manuscript was damaged, the outer
part of the first folio having been cut off and the writing obliterated by
dampness in many places, especially at the margins (see Kalbfleisch's
edition, p. VI). Restorations by Mynas were severely criticized by
Prantl (I, 591, 24n) and by Kalbfleisch in his preface.

The work is attributed to Galen in the superscription of the manuscript.
Nevertheless, Prantl (*ibid.*) regarded this attribution as false. Prantl's
arguments against the authenticity of the attribution rest, aside from an
apparent contradiction as to whether or not Galen had written commentaries on Aristotle's *Categories*, mainly on the contention that the
doctrine of the *Institutio* differs from logical doctrine stated in known
works of Galen and from logical rules actually followed by Galen in his
medical writings. Prantl, however, would date the work not long after
Galen, on the ground that it cites authors, e.g., Plato and Eratosthenes, in
a fashion that was not practiced after the middle of the third century.
I. von Mueller, in his work on Galen's *De Demonstratione*, accepts

Prantl's judgment but maintains that it contains many borrowings from an authentic work of Galen, which he conjectures to be *De Demonstratione*. Karl Kalbfleisch, finally, published in 1897 a paper vindicating Galen's right to be taken as the author (*Ueber Galens Einleitung in die Logik*). Kalbfleisch disposes of Prantl's principal argument by a careful study of the use and theory of logic in the rest of Galen's work and shows, contrary to Prantl, a close parallel both in doctrine and practice between the *Institutio* and many passages of Galen's authentic works.

Kalbfleisch's paper (*ibid.*) seems to me to have established conclusively that Galen is the author of the *Institutio*. Nevertheless, the doubts of earlier scholars had substance. Galen has left us two works listing in detail his writings on all subjects. (*De Libris Propriis* and *De Ordine Librorum*, Kuehn, XIX, 8–61.) Moreover, he frequently cites his own works in his other books. Yet there is no mention of the *Institutio* in any of his other works. On the other hand, there are writings included in the Galenic *corpus* that are universally admitted to be spurious. It seems, however, that these grounds for doubt are not as cogent as they appear at first. That he does not list the *Institutio* in his two bibliographical texts may be due to the fact that it was written later than they; as for the lack of citation in other works, this could be due to his treatment of the subject matter of the *Institutio* in his *De Demonstratione*, which he does cite over and over again and which he rightly considered a major work. By comparison the *Institutio* was a slight and elementary text for beginners. Most of the other spurious works are medical treatises that could easily be associated with the great medical authority in a later, uncritical age. Even the spurious *History of Philosophy* contains much medical lore and allusions to medical writers whom Galen cites in his genuine works. The subject matter of the *Institutio* is such that there seems little reason for a later age to attribute it to the man who was known as the theoretician of medicine, while in the generations immediately after Galen it is likely that people would have known his logical works well enough not to be misled if the work were not by Galen.

The MS. presents a text containing many barbarisms, which at first sight present evidence against Galenic authorship. But even Prantl was willing to ascribe these to a corrupt tradition. Kalbfleisch's edition has brilliantly corrected the text at many points, and now Mau, in his commentary and translation (*Galen, Einfuehrung in die Logik*), has put forward conjectural emendations that carry the work of Kalbfleisch still farther. As Kalbfleisch notes, the *Institutio* abounds in expressions that are part of Galen's usual expository vocabulary. In addition, the work is marked by the scorn of pedantry that is another of Galen's characteristics. One who spends time with the *Institutio* and then reads Galen's other works begins to recognize that the same mind is speaking in its pages as in the admittedly genuine works. Since Kalbfleisch's examination of the question is so inclusive, it is unnecessary to examine the authenticity of the work more closely in this introduction.

Taking it as proven, therefore, that the *Institutio* is the work of Galen, the question as to why it was not transmitted with Galen's other works arises. Here there is nothing to go on but guesswork. One obvious point is that Galen's reputation was based upon his medical work, and that the interest even in this was less in his scientific methods than in the supposedly factual information on physiology and diseases and their cure that was contained in the medical treatises. Most of his work on logic and scientific method was lost. What later ages sought from Galen was medical knowledge. The question thus becomes why this work was preserved at all. Here one might guess that as an elementary introduction to logic it acquired a vogue as a schoolbook and a copy fortuitously survived somewhere in the East, and was finally taken to the monastery where it was found.

To turn now to the purpose for which the *Institutio* was written, we are not given the direct help of the author, since the book lacks an introduction such as Galen commonly gave his readers. There are incidental remarks, however, scattered through the book which show that Galen intended to provide an outline of logic and meant it for beginners. We know, from Galen's own words in the bibliographical books already mentioned, that he often wrote expositions on particular scientific subjects for his friends, not intending them for public circulation. We know also, from the same source, that Galen was interested in scientific demonstration, that he considered a mastery of the logic of proof essential to the scientist, and that he had written many books and commentaries on logical subjects. His *De Demonstratione* was a *magnum opus*, in fifteen books. Even this did not satisfy him; he wrote several shorter works expanding some of the topics of *De Demonstratione*. Thus, it is conceivable that his lifelong interest in the subject together with his desire to help men acquire a proper scientific and professional training led him to write this book to meet the need of some young friend who was beginning a career in medical science. The simplicity and clarity of the book may have brought it to public attention and its usefulness as an introduction to formal logic may have given it a career, beyond Galen's expectations, in schools of philosophy and rhetoric. In this way it could have become separated from the medical works and persisted independently and could have come to rest finally on Mt. Athos. There is evidence of such an independent career enjoyed by *De Demonstratione*, collected by I. von Mueller (*Ueber Galens Werk vom Wissenschaftlichen Beweis*).

As for the intended readers, it is assumed that they have acquired a thorough Greek culture. Several times Galen, in explaining a term or an operation of logic, uses phrases such as "as the Greeks say" or "as anyone who speaks Greek knows" or similar expressions.   The examples he uses in illustrations, for instance, in explaining Aristotle's categories, assume a familiarity with the common cultural heritage of the Greek world—with the Peloponnesian War, or Hippocrates, or Eratosthenes. Galen also quotes Plato's *Alcibiades* and cites the fundamental analogy of the *Republic*, plainly assuming that his readers know them.   Toward the end of the book there is a reference to Posidonius, with no identifying description, again on the assumption that he needed no introduction to his readers.   All such references are confined to Greek culture and to a literary or at least bookish culture.   There are no references to Roman names and there are no contemporary references.

As already noted, the intended readers are assumed to be beginners in logic.   The content is built up from the fundamental epistemological ground of the distinction between immediate and deduced knowledge and the elementary terms are carefully explained.   Yet the readers are assumed to be serious students who will develop their knowledge by the use of exercise books.   They will also go on to more advanced studies, including *De Demonstratione*.

The people addressed by Galen, however, are not simply prospective logicians.   They are prospective scientists and medical men.   There is, however, evidence in Galen and from the existence of the work of Sextus Empiricus that medicine as a science was of interest to others than medical students and physicians.   Philosophers attended public anatomical dissections, for instance.   Therefore, the audience for this book need not have been restricted narrowly to professionals.   This view of his audience is supported by the fact that the text ignores or treats lightly questions having to do with the foundations of logic in favor of what he terms "usefulness for demonstration" (cf. *Inst. Log.*, ch. XIV, 8).   The book has, therefore, a practical aim.   It is to prepare students, or at least to begin their preparation, for a life devoted to work in science.   Demonstration plays a double role in science, in Galen's view.   On the one hand, it is useful in establishing facts, such as that the brain is the seat of sensation, and on the other hand, in refuting errors and carrying on controversies with the adherents of erroneous theories.   Galen throve on controversy, as almost any one of his works will testify.   He had an almost evangelical zeal for the true faith as given to men by Hippocrates. He found in mathematics a type of the compelling power of reason that was recognized as valid by the competing schools of dogmatic philosophy, schools that otherwise spent their time in vain disputation.   His *De Demonstratione* seems to have been an attempt to set forth a method that could supply sureness of knowledge, equal in certitude to mathematics, to fields other than that of number and figure.   Any man, therefore, who hoped to advance the boundaries of knowledge and to defend them against the incursions of ignorance had to be well grounded in logic.

The question of the state of the art of logic at the time the *Institutio* was written and how competently Galen has represented that state is next considered.   The *Institutio* presents an outline both of the moods and figures of the categorical syllogism, essentially as they are listed in Aristotle's *Prior Analytics*, and of the five indemonstrables of the hypothetical syllogisms, expressly attributed to Chrysippus, an attribution that is repeated in Sextus Empiricus (*Adv. Math.*, VIII, 223ff) and Diogenes Laertius (VII, 80–81), and is, therefore, to be considered authentic.   This division of the subject matter of logic was transmitted by Boethius, who wrote *De Syllogismis Categoricis* and *De Syllogismis Hypotheticis*, and passed on to the Middle Ages, to become the foundation on which modern logicians began their work.   In addition, however, Galen devotes several chapters of the *Institutio* to a presentation, not entirely coherent, of relational syllogisms.   Less is known about the earlier state of knowledge in regard to relational syllogisms, although it is obvious from Galen's discussion, from remarks in Alexander, and from scattered references in other authors such as Cicero, that the reasoning of the mathematicians had raised problems for the teachers of traditional logic.   It seems to follow from the confused state of Galen's presentation of these syllogisms that no Aristotle or Chrysippus had ordered them as adequately as these two had ordered the categorical and hypothetical forms respectively.   From the mention of Posidonius at the end of Galen's discussion and the quotation from him of a terminological name for a relational syllogism, as well as from Posidonius's known interest in mathematics, it may be inferred that he had done as much as anyone to set them in order.

Thus the content of the *Institutio* is largely made up of traditional material, whose form had been fixed since the fourth or third century B.C.   In the case of the Aristotelian material it is probable that Theophrastus and Eudemus, whose names are coupled in references of later writers, including Alexander and Boethius, were the systematizers of Aristotle's teaching.   (See Bochenski, *La Logique de Theophraste*, p. 125.)   The list of Chrysippus's writings on logic, as given in Diogenes (VII, 189–98), is so extensive that it looks as if there was little work to be done by his successors to systematize Stoic logic.   As has been remarked, relational logic, on the other hand, seems to have found no systematizer.

Two considerations should be kept distinct in speaking of a systematization of logic.   First, there is the more scientific task of working out all the implications of what the founder of the system first formulated, of filling in gaps that appear as further study is conducted, and of extending the range in one way or another.   This was the task of first-rate philosophers, such as Theophrastus.   (See Bochenski, *La Log.*, for an account of Theophrastus as a logician.)   Part of his accomplishment may have been the development of an adequate terminology to refer to the logical forms. The second kind of systematizing is the preparation of the material in a form suited to the use of students, graded according to difficulty so that the beginner can pass on to the stage of complete mastery. This was the work, no doubt, of countless unknown schoolmasters. It is likely that this kind of working over of the material did not get under way until the establishment of government sponsored schools in the early Empire. The list of Chrysippus's works suggests something of this sort, yet it also suggests that even works that seem to be elementary in content were exploratory in nature and thus transcended the pure type of textbook.

Each of these considerations has a bearing on the understanding of the *Institutio*; logical doctrines known to have been current in Galen's time assist in interpreting some of Galen's statements; conversely, passages from the work have been adduced in evidence of existing logical doctrine. Moreover, as regards the second consideration, something can be made of the technical vocabulary Galen uses to infer conclusions about the schoolmasters' technique for presenting logical material in elementary form; for instance, the naming of the four kinds of categorical propositions and the order in which the valid categorical syllogisms are given.

The first consideration is in every way the more important and therefore deserves a closer examination. One point leaps to the eye immediately: the historic rivalry between Peripatetic and Stoic logic. Galen presents many samples of their different terminologies as well as their contrasting forms of syllogisms, yet leaves one with the feeling that he or his sources do not give the full meaning of the controversy. The case, in fact, is not simple. The differences between the two schools are primarily metaphysical and are complicated by the fact that the Stoics combined originality with a large amount of borrowing or copying from other schools of thought, so that their distinctiveness is sometimes blurred. An example within the field of logic is the question whether Chrysippus's formulation of indemonstrable hypothetical syllogisms is original with him or is borrowed from Theophrastus. Prantl (I, 473ff) took the latter view, while Bochenski (*La Log.*, pp. 103ff) argues for the originality of the Stoics. The problem is wrongly viewed if it is considered simply as a question of historical priority. To judge from the fragmentary evidence, it is rather a question of how each author understood hypothetical syllogisms and this understanding is in each case a consequence of each man's metaphysics.

The fact that a Peripatetic logic and a Stoic logic can be spoken of as two distinct things results from the differing metaphysics of the two schools. In an oversimplified statement, Peripatetic logic has its point of view because Aristotle's metaphysics rests on the notion of a transcendent intellectual prime mover and an eternal world, while Stoic metaphysics presupposes a material divine Reason, the *hegemonikon*, Providence, immanent in a world destined to have an end.   The cycles of destruction and rebuilding amount, in effect, to positing a temporally finite world.

On the Peripatetic metaphysical presuppositions, the intellectual prime mover, "thought thinking itself," makes the world intelligible to the contemplative intellect.   For man, beginning his pathway to knowledge with the things of sense, real being and real knowledge belong to the immaterial forms of things.   That, for Aristotle, they are "in" things does not detract from their immaterial nature.   From the eternity of the world it follows that these forms of things belong to fixed classes.   In the moving, ever-changing world of sense, knowledge consists in discovering the unchanging forms of changing things.   Therefore, a knowledge which can be developed and increased by logical operations, as contrasted with the perfect knowledge of God, will be furthered by the logic of the categorical syllogisms.   Necessity abides in the relations of forms, i.e., in the relations of genera, species, properties, and attributes. The apodictic syllogisms necessarily yielding necessary conclusions from necessary premisses* thus brings man from the eternal flux of sense to the certainty of knowledge.   This knowledge, however, does not preclude the contingency of the future; there is room for chance in the causal order conceived by Aristotle.   So it is that hypothetical propositions and their syllogisms hold a subordinate place in the Peripatetic logic and are hypothetical in the sense that they express the radical contingency of uncertain futures.

On the other hand, hypothetical syllogisms take the most prominent place in the Stoic logic.   The Stoic God, who is immanent and is Providence in a finite world, causes the Stoics to make the center of their thinking the individual rather than the genus or species.   In Aristotle's eternal world are an infinite number of individuals, which are, therefore, knowable only in species, being undifferentiable in number.   For the Stoics, on the other hand, there must be a finite number of individuals in any one phase of the world cycle and the events in which they partake are finite and determined by Providence.   Therefore, knowledge consists of the necessary connectivity of events rather than of the necessary relation of genus and species.   It is characteristic of the respective philosophies that for Aristotle the ideal type of knower is the contemplative man, while for the Stoics he is the sage.   The Stoics did not ignore genera and species or categorical propositions, but they subordinated them to the chain of events and to hypothetical propositions and syllogisms. They replaced the Aristotelian categories, which are classes of predicates constructed on the model of genus and species, with a set of four categories, *substrate*, *quality*, *relation*, and *relation-in-a-certain-way*, which illustrate

* I follow the practice of some modern logicians who use this spelling to show that they are not talking about real estate.

the Stoic enchainment of things in that each succeeding category pre-supposes the preceding. (The argument offered in the preceding paragraphs owes much to A. Schmekel, *Die Positive Philosophie*, I, 522–25.)

There is a faint echo in the *Institutio* of what seems to have become a long rivalry between the two logics. Galen reports (*Inst. Log.*, ch. VII, 2) that the Peripatetic Boethos had asserted the Stoic position that the hypothetical syllogisms are prior to the categorical. For himself, Galen considers the controversy trivial. Yet J. Mau ("Stoische Logik," *Hermes*, vol. 85) has recently pointed out that for a long time, in fact until the revival of Aristotelianism in the first century B.C., Stoic logic held the field exclusively and the Peripatetic was forgotten. The Stoic marked, in Mau's view, what the world considered an advance, and the older logic came to have a merely historical interest and gradually was forgotten. Thus in the formative years of the Greco-Roman intellectual climate (i.e., the Hellenistic age), it was not so much Stoic logic as logic in the dimension first given it by Chrysippus that was looked upon as *the* science of logic and was the best known logic. The rediscovery of the technical works of Aristotle and the growth of the succession of com-mentators, of whom Alexander is the supreme example, restored the logic of Aristotle as a challenger to the prevailing logic and created the competition between Peripatetic and Stoic which finally brought about the downfall of Stoicism and the dominance during the Middle Ages of Aristotelian logic.

In another respect the notion of a fixed gulf between Stoic and Peripatetic logic is misleading. The term "logic" is partly to blame for the confusion. What is contrasted in Galen's *Institutio* is the Stoic and Peripatetic theory of syllogism, but for the Stoics the term logic is broader than this. When the Stoics maintain that the three branches of philosophy are ethics, physics, and "logic," their description of the content of these branches shows that the term logic has the broader meaning of all pertaining to the use of reason, including grammar, linguistics, semantics, epistemology, as well as what the modern world calls logic. (Von Arnim collects references to Chrysippus's logical opinions, which support this statement.) This latter is for the Stoics "dialectic" and includes, in general, the forms of reasoning to valid conclusions. Aristotle, of course, did not speak of "logic," but of "analytic" and, possibly, "apodictic."

The Stoics built on the Aristotelian beginning in grammar and logic in the broader sense. (A glance at the list of Chrysippus's works in Diogenes, Bk. VII, 189–98, already referred to will show that this is the case.) Much of the reason why their logic superseded Aristotle's *Organon* lay in the fact that they carried the analysis of linguistic and intellectual forms much further than did Aristotle, distinguishing elements of speech and thought more precisely, and inventing a technical vocabulary which made possible the systematic teaching of these subjects, even in an elementary way.   Thus the Stoics provided the knowledge for the text-books of the schools, which, under the Empire, were to make the knowledge of logic available to the ordinary educated man.

The work that produced the logical doctrine available in Galen's time, therefore, begins with the Stoic continuation of Aristotle's logical researches and then carries them forward in a different direction from Aristotle, largely as a result of a different metaphysical outlook.   But the forging of doctrine was influenced in the first century or two of Stoicism by another factor, the need to resist the skeptical assaults delivered against the Stoa by the New Academy.   This affected logical doctrine in two ways.   First, the battle was fought with the weapon of logic and, therefore, the defenders of Stoicism had to be sure that their troops were well trained in the use of this weapon; and, second, part of the attack consisted of an attempt to destroy the weapon itself and, therefore, forced the Stoics to take a closer look at the validity of their theories of reasoning and of proof.

The *Institutio* reflects some of this concern over the foundation of logic in its discussion of consequence and conflict as the basis of the hypothetical propositions and its criticism of Chrysippus's formulation of the five indemonstrable hypotheticals.   This has the appearance, as Schmekel points out (I, 530–32, also 536–37), of a later Stoic attempt to reformulate an acceptable Stoic position after Chrysippus's position had been weakened by the attack of Carneades or other Academics.

A closer look at Chrysippus's logic is in order here.   Galen, Sextus Empiricus, and Diogenes Laertius, as already cited, attest for him the formulation of a set of five "indemonstrable" hypothetical syllogisms. These are: a conditional major premiss with a minor affirming the antecedent or one denying the consequent; a negated conjunction in the major with a minor affirming one of its members; and a disjunction (exclusive alternation) with one member affirmed or denied in the minor premiss.

Precisely what Chrysippus's contribution was to the development of this important piece of logical doctrine is not easy to determine. Obviously, these five indemonstrables are in one sense simply a formulation of a kind of reasoning men use every day and had used for generations before Chrysippus.   Furthermore, Aristotle himself makes some use of hypothetical reasonings and calls attention to the need for further study of the subject (*Anal. Pr.*, 50a 40ff).   Theophrastus, according to many testimonies (see Bocheński *La Log.*), carried out some investigations into their nature.   Prantl (I, 385–88), stretching this evidence further than it will go, claimed for Theophrastus the complete formulation of the five indemonstrables.   Bocheński has shown that this is not the case and that Theophrastus systematized Aristotle's teaching on this as on other subjects, but that he did not free the hypotheticals from the pattern of thinking about logic that is found in the *Analytics*. This it seems is what Chrysippus was able to do. He was able to do it because he worked in the different metaphysical framework which Zeno had constructed as the foundation of Stoicism. For Theophrastus, the hypothetical propositions and their combinations in syllogisms were combinations of categorical propositions, by which more complex relations of things could be analyzed and made to yield conclusions. For Chrysippus, on the other hand, the combination of simple sentences in the hypotheticals made a new entity, a sentence that referred to a necessary conjunction or disjunction of events. The logical relations into which these sentences could enter therefore formed syllogisms of a different kind from the categorical syllogisms and permitted the analysis of different aspects of reality. The terminology of the two schools reflects this difference of opinion. Galen, in the *Institutio* (ch. III), tells us that the "old philosophers," meaning the Peripatetics, spoke of "hypotheticals by connection" and "hypotheticals by division," while the "younger" spoke of "conjunctions," i.e., conditionals, and "disjunctions," i.e., disjunctives or exclusive alternatives. The former mode of expression plays up the complexity of the sentences, the latter the unity. For Stoic logic, then, the affirmation that two predications are conjoined or disjoined is the element of the reasoning process rather than the affirmation that something is predicated of a subject.

Chrysippus did not arrive at his position at one stroke. The logic of conjunction and disjunction had several roots. On the one hand the Stoics devoted themselves to linguistic analysis and developed grammatical theory and terminology far beyond the rudimentary state to which the Peripatetics had brought them. Undoubtedly the analysis of the grammatical structure of the sentence, particularly of the forms of subordinate clauses, contributed to the fashioning of the hypothetical logic. On the other hand, reflection on the pioneer work of Aristotle in logic led to a closer scrutiny of the nature of inference. In the *Prior Analytics* Aristotle usually puts categorical syllogisms in the form of conditional sentences with the premises conjoined as antecedent and the conclusion as consequent. Thus the logical meaning of the conjunction "if" demanded attention. There are echoes in Sextus and Diogenes of a considerable discussion as to what constituted a valid inference. At any rate, something like the modern debate over formalistic logic seems to have developed in antiquity, with the Stoics gaining the credit or blame of being formalists. The *Institutio* reflects some of this discussion, and Galen lines himself up with the opponents of formalism, without, however, abstaining from presenting some of the formalistic doctrine, with criticism.

In the *Institutio* Galen criticizes Chrysippus's five indemonstrables on two grounds. First, he applies to them a criticism he frequently makes of Chrysippus, both in logical matters and in other scientific fields, that he pays more attention to verbal form than to the nature of the "facts" (*tois pragmasi*, ch. IV, 6), then he condemns the third indemonstrable (the negated conjunction) as useless for demonstration (ch. XIV, 8). He accepts Chrysippus's order of the indemonstrables but gives them a different interpretation. The first two, he says, have a major premiss expressing "complete consequence," the last two, "complete conflict," while the third is founded on "incomplete conflict." He goes on to add two more forms, starting from "incomplete consequence." He makes the meaning of these terms plain by defining "consequence" as possibility of being true together and conflict as not being true together. The property of completeness adds to agreement in truth (or disagreement) the further qualification, for consequence, that the members must also be false together, and for conflict that the two propositions that cannot be true together also cannot be false together. The incomplete forms may, for consequence, though true together, not necessarily be false together, while for conflict, they may be false together, even though they cannot be true together. Galen's treatment of conflict is more explicit than his treatment of consequence.

The doctrine of consequence and conflict is not original with Galen. It is briefly noted in Cicero's *Topica* (12, 53) and the words *akolouthia* and *mache* are attested as Stoic terms (e.g., Sextus, *Pyrrh.*, I, 184; II, 114). The words easily lent themselves to an informal characterizing of logical connection or incompatibility, but their use in constructing a scheme of the conclusiveness of logical forms is later than Aristotle. The scheme has obvious relations to the square of oppositions in the *De Interpretatione* and the theory of the convertibility of propositions, yet it goes beyond these two topics. It belongs to the Stoic view of hypothetical propositions as a new unity, rather than to the Peripatetic view that they are combinations of categorical propositions. Conversion and opposition are relations between separate categorical propositions; conflict and consequence are inherent in a single proposition and give it the power, when one of its member propositions is affirmed or denied, to yield a valid conclusion. The scheme must therefore have been worked out by reflection on Chrysippus's indemonstrables and must go along with the revision of Chrysippus's theory of the validity of inference which held that the consequent must be contained in the antecedent, if the inference is to be valid (see Sextus, *Adv. Math.*, VIII, 113ff). It is clear that this theory could easily lead to a conception of the conditional as an equivalence, and we shall see that some of Galen's treatment of the conditional implies this rather strongly. In general then, Galen's treatment reflects considerable movement in logical investigation in the first two centuries after Aristotle.

The *Institutio* treats not only the categorical syllogisms of Aristotle and the hypothetical syllogisms of Chrysippus together with the further development of these in the doctrine of consequence and conflict, but in its final chapters it deals with relational syllogisms and what in effect is a kind of mathematical logic. Galen may even be said to attest to the ancient recognition of the possibility of expressing universal propositions as quantified conditionals, a device beloved of modern symbolic logicians. At any rate, in his last chapter he mentioned a type of syllogism called "by additional assumption," which has as a major premiss, "Whatever A is predicated of, B is predicated of," which is equivalent to saying "If anything is A it is B," which is the conditional form of "Every A is B."

The treatment of the subject matter of the last four chapters is confused, showing that relational arguments had not found their Aristotle. The examples of relational arguments are partly mathematical but also are partly drawn from the kind of analogical presentation so common in the dialogues of Plato. In fact the fundamental analogy of the *Republic* is one of Galen's major examples of this kind of argument. Furthermore, Galen declares that these arguments and apparently all arguments derive their conclusiveness by coming under the "force" of (*kata dunamin*) an axiom. Possible light on Galen's meaning is shed by the passage (ch. XVI, 12) in which he speaks of sentences which are composed without the word "more," but with its force, i.e., sentences in which an adjective in the comparative degree occurs. It is possible that the expression with regard to the force of an axiom has the same meaning.

Galen attributes the "force of an axiom" phrase to Posidonius. This reference may be a clue to Galen's source for this part of his work. That Galen did not originate the doctrine of relational syllogisms is certain. Allusions in Cicero's *Topica* and in pseudo-Apuleius *De Interpretatione* as well as counterarguments in Alexander establish that the doctrine of these chapters was generally known, at least to those interested in logic. Yet there is no trace of such theorizing in Chrysippus. There is a discussion of the nature and use of axioms in Proclus's *Commentary on the First Book of Euclid*. Now much of the information in this work of Proclus is known to have been derived from Geminus, who was a disciple of Posidonius. It is therefore reasonably certain that the treatment in Galen of relational and mathematical arguments is ultimately derived in large part from Posidonius. The reference to him reads like a quotation from a man who is commenting on work that has previously been done and that he is systematizing. It is a possible hypothesis that Posidonius had interested himself in the work of professional mathematicians and had tried to generalize their method into a purely logical form. His authority may have been such as to lead to the incorporation of mathematical logic, thus generalized, into the logical tradition, which Galen, in turn, reproduces in the *Institutio*.

As a tentative summary of what has been said so far, it may be stated that between Aristotle and Posidonius the science of logic developed along several lines.   The work of Aristotle was systematized by Theophrastus, who mainly completed the analysis of the categorical propositions and the syllogisms constructed from them.   The Stoics, and especially Chrysippus, turned their attention, under the influence of Stoic metaphysics, to hypothetical syllogisms.   These, in turn, compelled thinkers to face the question of what is the nature of logical inference. Chrysippus's formalism did not satisfy his successors and, in the theory of consequence and conflict, a scheme was worked out to ground logical conclusiveness in the nature of things.   Meanwhile, the mathematicians had followed the lead of Euclid in trying to put their science on a logically firm foundation.   Their researches impressed Posidonius, especially because he gave reality to mathematical entities and thus was especially opposed to the formalism of Chrysippus.   So he may have generalized the logic of mathematics into a logic of relations dependent upon axioms and a realism as to logical relations, in opposition to the Stoic formalism.

It is thus probable that the system of logic we find embodied in Galen's *Institutio* had been completed by the middle of the first century B.C.   This conclusion is supported by the fact that we find traces of what is contained in all parts of the *Institutio* in Cicero, as well as by the fact that Galen's reference to a man later than the first century B.C., Boethus, seems to portray him as commenting on an established system rather than breaking new ground.

The *Institutio*, therefore, contains a body of doctrine about logic that represents a tradition that was several centuries in the making.   But, in addition to the theoretical matter of the book, it also reflects the pedagogic tradition by which the doctrines were put into a form for transmission to beginners.   Galen's book sets forth a developed technical terminology, one that shows how much care was spent in its construction, and, indeed, that it was worked out gradually in the course of discussion between the schools.   The book also shows how much stability had been achieved in the terms of logic.   The traditional names for the categorical propositions are there, in the form that they have retained to the present.   As already stated, the Peripatetic and Stoic divergences in terms for hypothetical propositions and for propositions in general are presented and explained. There is an air of fixity to these presentations, and to the order in which they occur, which makes it probable that Galen was taking over a formal language which had become well established.   This conclusion is borne out by a comparison with other works in which the same terms and doctrines occur, e.g., Cicero, *Topica* and ps.-Apuleius, *De Interpretatione*, where they occur in the same order and often with the same examples.

Yet there are parts of the book, scattered sentences, which have a flavor so characteristic of Galen that it seems certain he wrote the text

himself and did not copy from some existing handbook.   These sentences
are, first, references to his other works—especially *De Demonstratione*—
which show his constant awareness, while writing the *Institutio*, of the
large context in which it finds its locus.   Then there are definitions of
terms that are not strictly logical but are used in the definition or
explanations of logical terms, words such as *ennoia, hyphistemi*.   On
several occasions he shows his propensity for stating both sides of a
disputed point and then for taking a position above the dispute, saying
that it does not matter which view you take, as long as you understand
both views.   This is one of the points in which Galen shows his lifelong
conviction that the disputations of the sects must be transcended if one
is to reach the truth.   There are also a few claims to an independent
discovery.   One such is Galen's addition to the list of the ten categories
a new category of Composition.

The *Institutio* presupposes both the creative work in logic of the period
from Aristotle to Posidonius and the consolidating work of the schools.
How far does it indicate that Galen himself possessed special gifts in the
subject?   The orderly arrangement of the subject matter and the clarity
of its style tell very little about the qualifications of the book's author,
for clarity of style and orderly arrangement could both be no more than a
product of the cumulative labors of his predecessors in the field.   Logic
is almost by definition a begetter of clarity of style.   When, however, a
book exhibits not only an order that reflects a scholastic tradition but an
ordering of various such scholastic orders, it shows that its author has a
mastery of the subject that transcends the order imposed by the
tradition.

The book, moreover, gives evidence that Galen had a great interest in
questions of logic.   This is not only found in his references to other
works on logic but also in the fact that these references are working
references; that is, he gives them for readers who may wish to pursue the
subject further.   Clearly, then, Galen knows that logic is a subject
having depth to it and one that requires a good deal of hard work on the
student's part, if it is to be mastered.   Yet the tone of the book suggests
that this hard work is not unpleasant.   That Galen did, in fact, know
logic with some profundity is plain from the list of his writings on the
subject and from the length of his *De Demonstratione* and from the pride
with which he refers to this book, as well as from the use he makes of
logical forms in his non-logical writings.

There is no doubt that Galen was competent in logic, but the question
is rather as to how far his insight into logic extended.   His competence is
certainly far greater than that of a text book writer, yet it falls short of the
originality of a Theophrastus or a Chrysippus, not to mention Aristotle.
His interest is directed to the usefulness of logic in scientific demonstration.   This is not to say that he had a practical rather than a theoretical

interest in logic.   For him, usefulness for proof is a theoretical criterion to be used in establishing the validity of logical forms.

The question of Galen's relation to theoretical logic leads on to the question of his relation to philosophy in general.   Galen was, of course, a professional medical man, both a practicing physician and a scientist who engaged in teaching and research or experimentation.   He began his education, however, with the study of philosophy.   His father and grandfather were well versed in mathematics, and his father encouraged him to study philosophy, as he did for two years with the best teachers then living in the Eastern Mediterranean area.   In his seventeenth year, however, he abandoned philosophy for medicine, and in medicine he made his career.   His desertion of philosophy, nevertheless, did not make him anti-philosophical, quite the contrary!   Most of his works testify to his continued linking of philosophy with his scientific work. Indeed, he couples the terms philosopher and physician so often as to suggest that the compound phrase stood for a single concept, a single profession.

Galen has been classified as an eclectic in philosophy, but the student of Galen cannot accept this judgment.   He was neither trying to patch together a philosophy from different sources, nor to summarize philosophical thinking, as Cicero was.   He had a clear grasp of the fact that philosophy had trained the minds of men to look rationally at the world and to try to interpret it in rational terms.   He saw that none of the sects could offer a final interpretation and that, having cemented the views of their founders into dogmas, they too often engaged in vain disputes about the truth of these dogmas and lost sight of the philosophical prerequisite for the attainment of truth.   This Galen found in the methods of logic as exemplified most purely in the work of the mathematicians.   His program for himself, as he developed it in the course of his growth in his profession, was to establish the science of medicine firmly on the solid accomplishments of Hippocrates, enlarged and completed by the work of philosophically trained investigators like himself.   Philosophy as a way of life had been the dominant view of the sects.   This view was inspired, no doubt, by the image of Pythagoras and the preaching of Plato and Aristotle and was confirmed by the practice of the Stoics and the Epicureans.   Galen, a worldly man of the age of the Antonines, conceived philosophy less as a way of life than as a body of authoritative opinion about the nature of the world.   Galen exemplifies the type of man who flourished under the early Empire, the man of talent who makes his way from the provinces to a position of prominence in the capital of the world.   He shows a likeness to the provincial emperors, the talented and competent administrators who used their knowledge of how the imperial machine ran to make their way to power and to rescue the Roman world from the recurrent crises brought on by misgovernment.   Galen, however, was competent in the world of the mind. He applied his knowledge of the machine of philosophy and science to the task of bringing order into the teaching and practice of medicine. He accepted as given the philosophical principles that the long dialectic of the schools had established most firmly, just as the soldier-emperors accepted the legal and political principles that the Romans had worked out in their experience. What he did was to make those principles work for his day and age, to codify under those principles the empirical knowledge that medicine in its progress had discovered, and to set forth the rules of operation for the transmission of that knowledge and for its enlargement. It is to this latter end that his work in logic is directed. The *Institutio* is one part, the introductory part, of this codifying and unifying work.

Analysis of the
Institutio

The *Institutio* raises so many questions about the sources from which Galen drew his material and about his relation to this material, that a general survey of the work is desirable. Most of the questions are dealt with in detail in the commentary. Here a rounded view of their relation to the book as a whole will be undertaken.

As previously pointed out, the main topic of the work is the syllogism in its various forms: the categorical, the hypothetical, and the "relational." The material concerning the first form derives from Aristotle's *Prior Analytics*, with minor changes. Similarly, the treatment of the hypothetical syllogisms is based on the five indemonstrables, whose formulation we know is due to Chrysippus. The chapters dealing with relational syllogisms point to no such well-organized source. The examples Galen gives under this heading are cited in Alexander in different portions of his commentary on the *Prior Analytics* as if they were desultory discoveries of later logicians, apparently Stoics for the most part, and as if they were not brought under a single heading. In treating these Galen makes a claim to originality, whether of nomenclature or theory is not clear.

This basic material is embedded in preparatory explanations and additional comment. The analysis of arguments into propositions and of propositions into terms leads Galen to begin his work with the elucidation of these elements. Moreover, the fact that a technical language for logic had been elaborated by Aristotle and his successors and, after them, the Stoics, caused Galen to include at appropriate places definitions of these technical terms and comments on the different terms used by Peripatetics and Stoics for the same or similar logical forms. In addition, Galen indulges a tendency, rather marked in all his works, to define incidental terms that he uses in the course of his exposition.

The structure and content of the work must be examined against the background of the traditions within which Galen worked. Unfortunately there is no closely similar work with which to compare it. Its title

proclaims it an *Eisagoge*, an introduction to logic.   Galen himself calls
it an *hypographe*, an outline, as distinguished from a detailed exposition
(ch. XI, 2).   There is no other such introduction to logic preserved from
the logical writers of antiquity, although ps.-Apuleius, *De Interpretatione*
comes closest to it in form and content.   That there were many such
introductions is indicated by a passage in Aulus Gellius and by one in
Proclus's commentary on the first book of Euclid.   In *Attic Nights*,
XVI, 8, 1, we read:

> Cum in disciplinas dialecticas induci atque imbui vellemus,
> necessus fuit adire atque cognoscere quas vocant dialectici *eisagogai*.

and in Proclus, *in Euclid*, p. 193, Friedlein:

> Kai hoi ge apo tês Stoas hapanta logon haploun apophatikon
> axiôma prosagoreuein eiôthasin, kai hotan dialektikas hêmin graphou-
> sin technas, "peri axiômatôn," touto dia tôn epigrammatôn dêloun
> ethelousin.

It is clear that the rest of the chapter in Gellius discusses Stoic terminology and that his "dialectici" are Stoics or writers drawing on the
Stoic tradition in logic.   These two passages imply that the production
of introductions and handbooks of logic was a thriving industry among
the Stoics.

Perhaps, in view of Mau's contention, in the Hermes article already
referred to, that logic had become standardized by the last century before
Christ and that there was not a clear-cut distinction between the logic of
the rival schools, it would be more proper to attribute the industry of
writing handbooks to the "dialectici" and assume that these men, whoever
they were, drew their material from Chrysippus and his followers, with
some reference back to Theophrastus.   Albinus's summary of "dialectic"
in chapters 5 and 6 of his *Introduction to Platonic Dialogues* (*Platonis
Dialogi*, Teubner, VI, 156ff) is an example of this kind of thing, with
rather heavier emphasis on Peripatetic contributions to logic.   The
handbooks came into being, no doubt, to satisfy different demands.
Some would have been written by Stoics for Stoics, especially after the
Roman government undertook to support professors of each of the
philosophical schools in the principal cities of the Empire.   Others
would perhaps have served the teachers of rhetoric and of jurisprudence.
Galen's book, at any rate, is an actuality.   As has already been suggested,
it may have been unique among introductions because of its author's
independence of the schools and his orientation towards demonstration.

As an introductory outline, however, Galen's book does not deal with
the fundamentals of logic.   It would be wrong to describe it as either
Peripatetic or Stoic, if these two terms connote a sharp difference of
opinion about the nature and purpose of logic.   Galen stands apart from
the philosophical sects and above them, as has already been said.

Whether there were logic books before Galen adopting the same neutral stand cannot be discovered. Most of the information we have concerning the material treated by Galen comes from Diogenes, Alexander, Sextus, and, to a lesser extent, from Plutarch. From none of these men do we have a systematic exposition of logic on any level. Diogenes, of course, gives valuable doxographic material derived from Diocles. Alexander wrote commentaries on Aristotle, as a Peripatetic and "second Aristotle;" his treatment of Stoic material is polemical; Sextus is equally polemical from the Skeptic position; Plutarch's references to logic are incidental to his main philosophical purpose and he is, of course, a Platonist. Accordingly, while remarks of all these authors are of benefit in the elucidation of many particular statements in the *Institutio*, they are of little help in explaining the work as a whole.

The general form is dictated by the nature of the material and is, in fact, exhibited by any elementary textbook on logic, including the most recent textbooks of symbolic logic. Alexander has described this necessary form in his commentary on the *Prior Analytics* (p. 9, l. 25): "Since the discussion of the syllogism is necessary for the discussion of demonstration, as we have already said, and since the syllogism is composed of premisses and the premisses of terms, with good reason he discusses these things, from which the syllogism gets its being, before talking about the syllogism." But this general form is complicated for Galen by the fact that he gives the terminology of both Peripatetics and Stoics. He must, therefore, combine his definitions of terms and propositions with a listing of the different names used for these elements by the two schools. His task is further complicated by the fact that he undertakes to introduce the reader to three kinds of syllogism: the categorical, the hypothetical, and the relational. Here the complexity of the subject becomes even greater, since, although the categoricals belong to the Peripatetics and the hypothetical to the Stoics, by right, one might say, of Prior Elaboration, adherents of each school had worked with both kinds of syllogisms. There are, therefore, both terminological duplications to be taken into account and also theoretical differences to be noticed. Although the latter are of little interest to Galen in this book, they underlie his treatment and occasionally call for comment. Finally, the third class of syllogism, because it had not been thoroughly worked out and presents in our sources a grab-bag appearance, seems to have required of Galen more original work in arranging his exposition than the other two classes.

If one may venture a theory of the composition of the book, it is this: Galen has at hand, through one source or another, the standardized version of the categorical syllogisms as derived from the *Prior Analytics* but reduced to school jargon form, and similarly such a version of the syllogisms of Chrysippus. Perhaps these versions were already combined into one text.   He was familiar with disputes between the schools about interpretations of the form and significance of the syllogisms.   The terms *palaioi* or *archaioi* and *neoteroi* were already stereotyped designations for the parties in dispute, showing that the division had become rigid by Galen's time.   As an expert in the theory of demonstration, Galen feels himself qualified to judge many of the points in dispute in reference to a rather practical standard of usefulness for demonstration, that is, usefulness to the practicing scientist.   And lastly, many of his statements in the *Institutio* and his ways of exposition stem from personal traits, particularly his genuine love of teaching, his sympathy with learners, and his didactic habit of emphasizing a point by repeating it three times.

The *Institutio*, therefore, is not a compilation or an epitome but a genuine composition of the author, an original work, in the sense that Galen has selected his material with his mature understanding of logic always in control, and he has interwoven with it comments of his own, designed to emphasize what he finds important for the student of science to know.   The book has interested students of logic since its rediscovery, primarily as a source of knowledge about ancient logic.   It can be of equal interest to those who would like to see the quality of the mind of a scientist of the age of the Astonines.   From it a good understanding of the culture both of a man and of an age emerges.

A careful reading of the *Institutio* makes possible at least a tentative apportionment of the material between that which Galen took from standard sources and that which he contributed of his own.   Owing to the inadequacy of our sources for ancient logic, no certain line between these parts can be drawn.   The following paragraphs are an attempt to sketch this probable apportionment.   Detailed justification of some of the opinions offered will be presented in the commentary.

There are certain indications to be followed in the attempt to place particular sections of text.   Foremost among these is the terminology, which Galen distinguishes as Peripatetic and Stoic.   Then the illustrative examples which appear practically verbatim in other authors show not only where Galen is drawing on already formulated statements but also whether these statements come from a Peripatetic or a Stoic source. For instance, the type-names Dion, Theon, and Philon and the example "night or day" are found often in Stoic sources, while "Socrates" or propositions about virtue, justice, and honor bespeak the Peripatetics.   A further means of discriminating parts, which must, however, be used judiciously, lies in the style of the sentences.   Those sections which derive from standardized formulations are expressed in a terse sentence structure, worn smooth by constant repetition; when Galen is offering a comment or explanation of his own, the style is more lively, although sometimes a little less clear (Galen is generally a clear writer).   A pattern seems to be exhibited in some of his chapters: the first part presents the material taken from a source; this part is followed by remarks of the author. Lastly, as in his other works, Galen makes fairly frequent digressions. His habit of digression was a minor vice and he is aware of it, once scolding himself after he has made a long one (ch. XIV, sec. 9).

With these guide posts in mind, one may attempt, at last, an analysis of the book.

The first chapter would seem to be Galen's own composition. The opening statement of the difference between self-evident knowledge and demonstrated truth, although a commonplace since Aristotle, is in verbal accord with remarks Galen makes in other works (partly, of course, because of Kalbfleisch's conjectures based on these other passages) and there can be little doubt that Galen penned the sentence himself. The sentence in the second section which makes a general statement about the effect of demonstration on a respondent is obviously an independent construction, otherwise it would be clearer. (Here again emendation by Kalbfleisch is present. Mau in his translation omits the sentence, considering it hopelessly corrupt.) Then the example of a demonstrative argument, though derived from a Stoic source, has been chosen for this place with independence of thought. We meet the same example in Alexander, illustrating an entirely different point and expressed somewhat differently (*in Anal. Pr.*, p. 21, Wallies). The elaboration of the example could be characteristic of Galen's prolixity. The last two sections also are in Galen's individual style. Although they simply define the terms argument, conclusion, and premiss, they show Galen's fondness for comparing different terms for the same thing, and they also contain addresses to the reader, second persons of verbs, that are signs of his pedagogical manner and are not found in sections that are clearly repeating standard texts.

Chapter II deals with the categorical propositions. It classifies them in two ways: one by means of subject matter, the other by form; and it analyzes the composition of the latter out of terms. The style of the chapter suggests that Galen is working from a text, possibly one of the introductions *peri axiômatôn* mentioned by Proclus. The technical terms are mostly Peripatetic, e.g., *protasis* for proposition, *horos* for term; but the name "Dion" and the grammatical word *epirrhema* look Stoic, while the name "categorical" for a kind of proposition is at least post-Aristotelian. (Mau *ad loc.* conjectures it is Galen's own coinage.) Since the Stoics adopted much of the Peripatetic elementary logic, this combination does not preclude a Stoic source.

The first section classifies categorical propositions by subject matter in an odd way. In Kalbfleisch's text an example of an affirmative proposition and its corresponding negation is given for each of the ten Aristotelian categories, preceded by a pair of existential propositions, which do not, as in the other cases, have the same subject. The implication is that the

term "categorical" was given to the proposition because such propositions
had predicates from one or another of the categories.   This point is
discussed in the commentary.   Similarly, the pairing of affirmative and
negative propositions calls to mind the apparent school exercises of the
Papyrus Letronii *peri apophatikôn* (von Arnim, II, no. 180).   Lastly, the
subject matter is encyclopedic in nature and thus points to a source of
the later period, when encyclopedic compilation of knowledge became
common.   All these considerations indicate that Galen may here be
following a textbook that drew on a source giving a Stoic version of
Peripatetic doctrine.

The content of the rest of the chapter is consonant with this theory.
The discussion of terms is conducted in a language that uses a fully
developed grammatical vocabulary, while the discussion of universal,
particular, and singular propositions not only shows that the conventional
names for these propositions are fully established but that they are
beginning to have a well-worn look.   The distinction between proper
and common names is made deftly and routinely, relying on the distinction
between divisible and indivisible terms, but without insistence, as if the
language of genus, species, and individual had long been settled.   The
statement that particular negatives have two equivalent forms may be an
addition of Galen's own, since he had written a book, *On Equivalent
Propositions*, and elsewhere in this book shows an interest in the subject.

In Chapter III Galen takes up hypothetical propositions.   Here the
material seems to be somewhat original with the author.   He gives two
sets of names for propositions of this sort, one Peripatetic, the other Stoic,
or at least used by the *neoteroi* who in this context seem to be Stoics.   He
also digresses to discuss the meaning of some auxiliary terms.   He
concludes the chapter with a criticism of those who pay more attention to
verbal expression than to the facts signified; these again are the Stoics.
The sentiment is dear to Galen and reflects his continuing struggle for
relevance against meaningless disputes between sects.   A pendant to this
last section is a mention of two equivalent forms for the disjunctive
proposition.   It seems a fair conclusion that Galen has reworked the
material of this chapter and has put more of his own opinions into it than
into the preceding chapter.

Chapter IV continues the exposition of hypothetical propositions and
connects them with the doctrine of consequence and conflict.   If more
were known about this doctrine, it would be easier to assess Galen's
originality here.   At any rate, Galen writes with some feeling in this
chapter and criticizes Chrysippus by name and severely.   (Dr. Edelstein
has pointed out to me that this criticism is often an indication of a reference
to Posidonius, who was very much opposed to Chrysippus.   Posidonius
figures in the *De Hippocratis et Platonis Placitis*, which is in great part a
diatribe against Chrysippus.)   Here Galen introduces a criticism of the

third indemonstrable of Chrysippus, a matter of some importance to him, since he returns to it again with emphasis when he discusses the hypothetical syllogisms. Again he ends the chapter with a note on usage which reads as if it were his own. This chapter, too, seems to be more Galen's than a transcription from a textbook source.

The discussion of hypothetical propositions is carried on into Chapter V on a less elementary level. The disjunctive is connected with the notion of "conflict;" then three different types of disjunctives are named, the third, the "paradisjunctive," turning out to express "incomplete consequence." The discussion is partly confused by introducing propositions consisting of disjunctions of more than two members. Galen is led on by this turn of the discussion to anticipate treatment of the five indemonstrables, which, strictly speaking, belong later in the book. The paradisjunctive interested him especially. Twice later he returns to it. The term, apparently, was used in various senses by different authors and Galen may have wanted his understanding of it, which is a quite competent understanding, clearly established for his readers. (Mau, in his commentary, adopts a different view of what the paradisjunctive meant for Galen from that expressed here. Mau's interpretation, especially of Chapter XV, is attractive, but I shall continue to hold to my interpretation.) In this chapter, then, Galen seems to have taken existing material, some of it containing conflicting doctrines, and developed it according to an understanding of his own. From one point of view the chapter is a long digression on the meaning of the term "disjunctive" and thus is an example of one of Galen's favorite devices.

In Chapter VI Galen returns to the accepted order of treatment, when he takes up conversion of propositions and syllogisms. He first deals with conversion of both kinds of propositions, then with conversion of syllogisms, especially the rule used by Aristotle for reduction *per impossibile*. The material of the first five sections is standard and most of it comes ultimately from Aristotle's *Prior Analytics*. But in sections 6 and 7 Galen has appended comment of his own; in section 6 he remarks that the rules of conversion apply also to "*tropoi*;" he then feels the need of explaining this term. It means, he tells us, hypothetical syllogisms expressed schematically with ordinal numerals standing for the propositions in the syllogisms. This leads him once more to list the five indemonstrables. Section 7 returns to the paradisjunctive, which is not one of the premises of any of the five indemonstrables. So again Galen follows his pattern of giving additional comment after first presenting accepted doctrine.

In Chapter VII Galen goes on with the digression on hypothetical syllogisms and gives two descriptive terms that are applied to them. Then he refers to a discussion of the relative priority of categorical and hypothetical syllogisms, cites opinion on each side of the question, and, true to his principle of standing above the battle, announces that in his view the argument is irrelevant.   In section 4 he takes up the categorical syllogisms and the rest of the chapter is straight listing and exemplification of the three figures.   The next four chapters list the valid moods of each of the three figures and, in Chapter XI, the further inferences and indirect moods possible in addition to the moods of the three figures. Nowhere, incidentally, is the "Galenic" fourth figure mentioned.   In these chapters he follows regulation Peripatetic doctrine, with little excursion into bypaths, little or no development of original points of view.

Chapters XII and XIII discuss the subjects in which the categorical syllogisms are useful for demonstration and which syllogisms are useful for which different purposes.   Usefulness for demonstration is the most important thing about syllogisms for Galen and once more the style betrays more feeling.   He takes up again the supposed connection between categoricals and categories and he gives another encyclopedic list of subjects of investigation under the ten categories.   Here, moreover, Galen makes a definite claim to originality, asserting that he has himself added the category of "composition," which had been overlooked by Aristotle.

Chapter XIV takes up, now in proper order, the hypothetical syllogisms. In this chapter he makes the interesting assertion that the hypothetical syllogisms are useful for questions of existence, such as, "Do the gods exist?"   "Is there a void?".   As opposites of the categorical syllogisms, the hypotheticals must, in Galen's opinion, deal with questions that transcend the categories.   Galen does not adhere very strictly to this rule.   In places in his other works he offers demonstrations of a certain opinion both by means of a categorical syllogism and a hypothetical (see, for instance, *De Semine*, Kuehn, IV, 609).   The main part of the chapter, however, is concerned with the five indemonstrables of Chrysippus. Galen repeats what he has said in the earlier part of the book.   Again he calls attention to the different vocabularies of Peripatetics and Stoics. He then proceeds to offer as his own a set of five indemonstrables, based on the kinds of consequence and conflict, and differing from Chrysippus's especially in the theory of the third one of the group.   He discourses at length upon this difference, and finally recalls himself, with an apology, from his digression.   It is to be observed that he claims as his the theory he presents, asserting that his forms are only verbally similar to those of Chrysippus.   One of his rare first person verbs occurs at the end of section 5 of this chapter.   The value of his claim is uncertain.   The question will be discussed in the commentary when the topics of consequence and conflict are treated.   For the present purpose it is enough to note that the claim to originality precludes the chapter's being a mere transcription.

Chapter XV bears the clearest evidence of Galen's originality.   It is
devoted to the paradisjunctive, which Galen (if Kalbfleisch's editing of the
first sentence is sound) explains as based on incomplete consequence.
We have seen his two earlier statements (ch. V, 1 and ch. VI, 7) about the
paradisjunctive proposition.   Here he discusses the syllogisms that have
that proposition as a major premiss.   What marks the treatment as
largely original is, first, that his concept of the paradisjunctive is more
clearly defined than the reference to it in Aulus Gellius, XVI, 8, and,
second, that the example given to illustrate the syllogisms is a physio-
logical one, dealing with the kind of question frequently encountered in
Galen's medical works (see *De Fac. Nat.*, II, ch. vii).   Furthermore, the
amount of space he devotes to the forms shows that he believed it was
something new and would not be easily understood.   Then the two
paradisjunctive syllogisms increase the number of such syllogisms from
Chrysippus's five to seven, although he had said nothing in his treatment
of the latter, derived, no doubt, from a standard source, to prepare the
reader for this increase.   It may be, however, that he did not think that
these two syllogisms were indemonstrable, although he says nothing about
their being derivable from the five.   (Note, however, that Mau, reading a
different text, takes a radically different view of this chapter.)   At the
end of the chapter he gives an example from Plato of an argument
possibly in this form.   Since this is not a stock example he seems to have
selected it himself, although, possibly, he owes it to Posidonius, whose
influence begins to appear in the next chapters.

Chapters XVI, XVII, and XVIII seem to be more original than some
of the earlier parts of the book.   They deal with relational syllogisms.
Galen explains why he chose the term relational and then gives an account
of how he came to recognize that relational syllogisms depend for their
force on a general axiom.   The examples he gives are paralleled in
Alexander (e.g., *Anal. Pr.*, pp. 21–22), by whom they are attributed to
the *neoteroi* or the Stoics, so that Galen's claim is not to the discovery of
these syllogisms.   I would rather refer it to the interpretation of them
and to the recognition that though they play a part in mathematical
reasoning they extend to non-mathematical objects.   According to
Alexander, the Stoics called these forms "unmethodically concluding."
Galen refers to this term in his last chapter, obviously taking it to refer to
some other types of argument than he discusses under relational syllogisms.
So perhaps Galen's originality lies in according to the forms of relational
syllogisms a more rational status than other writers on logic had been
willing to grant.

Chapter XIX is a brief rejection of certain forms handed down in the
tradition, some Peripatetic, some Stoic, as not being, strictly, forms of
argument at all.   Since some of these same forms are referred to by
Alexander as if they were valid to some degree, or as if there was respectable

opinion that held them to be so, this rejection of them must be taken as Galen's own judgment.

It is hoped that the foregoing sketch of the contents of the *Institutio* offers a basis for the following conclusions: the work follows, in general, the traditional order of treatment of the syllogistic branch of logic; much of its material is drawn from a standard textbook of logic in which an attempt was made to give both Peripatetic and Stoic formulations; this was not done with a view to reconciling conflicting theories, but in the belief that there was a single science of logic to which both the Peripatetics and the Stoics had contributed, with, it is true, some difference of terminology that had to be reconciled; Galen worked freely with this material, making comments of his own, and, in particular, carrying on his feud with Chrysippus; furthermore, Galen believed that he had made some discoveries of his own in logic, and he presents them in appropriate places; he is himself neither a Peripatetic nor a Stoic, but because of his dislike of Chrysippus and his familiarity with Plato and Aristotle, he tends to use a vocabulary that has more affinities with the Peripatetic than with the Stoic, although in dealing with the Stoic contributions he uses the Stoic terms interchangeably with the Peripatetic. Finally, because of his habit of digressing when a particular point interests him, the book offers many interesting side lights on the thought of the age of consolidation in which he lived and which, in large part, he made.

There is possibly an alternative conclusion to this analysis. The bulk of the material of the *Institutio* and its arrangement may have already been fixed before Galen's time by a single hand. This supposition would not detract from Galen's individuality in preparing this document, in the sense that he contributed comments of his own or that he knew the subject and knew how he wanted to convey it. It would, however, account for the similarity of some of the ordering of the material to things that appear in Cicero's *Topica* and Apuleius's *De Interpretatione*. It would also give a plausible reason for the references to bits of factual information seeming to reflect the state of knowledge of the first century B.C. and very little that was later than that.

If the supposition of an earlier hand shaping the material of the *Institutio* is considered seriously, then an obvious candidate for identification as that hand is Posidonius. In the first place Galen was familiar with the works of Posidonius. In the fourth and fifth books of the *de Placitis Hippocratis et Platonis* Posidonius is frequently cited as a witness against Chrysippus and several passages are quoted from his book, *peri pathôn*. From these citations it is clear that Posidonius was a severe critic of Chrysippus, so that the strictures against the latter that occur in the *Institutio* might very well be Posidonian.

Secondly, there is the last sentence of Chapter XVIII of the *Institutio*, which attributes to Posidonius the naming of a class of relational syllogisms as "conclusive with the force of an axiom." The meaning of the phrase may be left for the commentary. The sudden introduction of Posidonius's name here fits in best with the hypothesis that he has been in Galen's mind all the time. Now at the end of the treatment of logic he acknowledges his dependence.

That Posidonius treated of logical matters is clear from references in Diogenes Laertius. In particular, the last sentence of Book VII, ch. 54, "Alloi de tines tôn archaioterôn Stôikôn ton orthon logon kriterion apoleipousin, hôs ho Poseidônios en tôi Peri kritêriou phêsi," shows that he held a view of the foundations of logical thinking that is consistent with the view attributed to him in the *Institutio*.

The chapters of the *Institutio* dealing with relational syllogisms illustrate them with examples from arithmetic and geometry. Galen more than once refers to Posidonius's knowledge of mathematics. For instance in *Hippocrates and Plato* (Kuehn, p. 390) he says, "Posidonius, trained in geometry and more accustomed than the other Stoics to follow demonstrations . . . ." Cicero also, in *De Natura Deorum*, II, 88, tells us that Posidonius had made a mechanical model that illustrated the motions of the sun, moon, and five planets. Therefore, there is nothing implausible in Posidonius's having elaborated the doctrines of relational syllogisms as they are found in Galen's final chapters.

Proclus's commentary on the first book of Euclid (edited for Teubner by Friedelein, p. 199) attests a book by Posidonius attacking Zeno the Epicurean's denial of the possibility of logical demonstration. The context shows that the issue between Posidonius and the Epicurean was, in effect, the validity of mathematical reasoning. The remark quoted by Galen in the *Institutio* could very well have been a part of such a discussion. However, it is more likely that it came from the *peri kritêriou*. This would most likely be the case if most of the content of the *Institutio* was drawn from Posidonius and not just the latter portion, the discussion of relational syllogisms.

It is a commonplace of the history of philosophy that Posidonius was a Platonizing Stoic and that he was aware of Aristotle and respectful of his position. This statement is supported by numerous references in Galen's *de Placitis Hippocratis et Platonis*. (See for instance, p. 396 of Mueller's edition of this work or p. 401 of the same edition.) Therefore, the combination of Aristotelian and Stoic logic that the *Institutio* sets forth could very well have been already worked out by Posidonius.

A final point may be made. In Sextus Empiricus's *Against the Logicians* (Bk. I, sec. 93, which I cite under the general title *Adversus Mathematicos*) there is a quotation from Posidonius embedded in a discussion of the Pythagorean view that number is the *logos* which is the fundamental "criterion" of knowledge. As translated by Bury it reads: "Just as light is apprehended by the luciform sense of sight, and sound by the aeriform sense of hearing, so also the nature of all things (*hê tôn holôn phusis*) ought to be apprehended by its kindred reason (*tou logou*)."

If this quotation is authentic it goes far in explaining the phrase "by force of an axiom." The ground of logical validity is found in nature, the nature of the soul and its kinship with the nature of the universe. Of course, since the sentence is quoted from an exposition of Plato's *Timaeus*, it may represent Posidonius's interpretation of Platonic doctrine and not his own. Still it is not out of keeping with what we know of Posidonius's opinions and interests.

There is a little more to the quotation. Since it is embedded in a passage about Pythagoreans it may be that Sextus felt that Posidonius's views on number were similar to the Pythagoreans' views. If so, the largely numerical cast of Galen's chapters on relational syllogisms might stem directly from Posidonius.

This alternative conclusion would leave Galen in his role as organizer of a scientific curriculum for his age and posterity. It would attach him closely to the Posidonian tradition and help light some corners of that tradition.

Translation of
Galeni,
Institutio Logica

Chapter I*

1* As human beings, we all know one kind of evident things through sense perception and another through sole intellectual intuition; and these we know without demonstration; but things known neither by sense perception nor by intellectual intuition, we know through demonstration.

2 The finding of things known through demonstration has to come from things already known, but not just simply so, from any chance prior knowledge, but from knowledge of things that are proper to what is sought to be demonstrated; since indeed, in any subject under discussion, we can, on the basis of some appropriate argument, persuade a man who can be compelled to agree to this argument; for example, if we happen to agree that Theon is equal to Dion and that Philon is equal to the same Dion; obviously, it will follow from these premisses that Theon is equal to Philon, through the proposition that things equal to the same thing are also equal to one another.

3 This demonstration, you see, consists of three parts; first, the first thing said, which was: "Theon is equal to Dion"; second, the following statement: "Philon is equal to Dion"; and third, in addition to these: "Things equal to the same thing are also equal to one another"; and it will be concluded from them that Theon is equal to Philon.

4 This latter is what is called a "conclusion"; but those sentences from which, on their being assumed, this is concluded are each called an "assumption"; and the entire form of speech through which, when

* Chapter and section numbers follow Kalbfleisch's edition.

certain things are agreed to, a conclusion is inferred, is itself called both a "conclusion" and a "syllogism"; but notice that one may properly disregard those who call the conclusion in the strict sense a syllogism.

5   If, moreover, having some prior knowledge, either through perception or demonstration, we propose some statement about the nature of things, let this statement be called a "premiss"; for this was the usual term among the ancients; but if it is a proposition carrying conviction of itself to the intellect, they gave it the name "axiom"; e.g., "Things equal to the same thing are also equal to one another." You must not quarrel with those who name all declarative sentences of every kind "axioms," but, having learned their custom, accept them as speaking in the way they wish.

Chapter II

1   Some premisses make statements about simple existence, as when you say, "There is Providence," "There is no centaur"; or they make statements about substance, as in the following examples: "The air is a body," "The air is not a body"; and about magnitude: "The sun is a foot wide"; "The sun is not a foot wide"; some concerning quality: "The sun is hot by nature"; "The sun is not hot by nature"; and some about relation: "The sun is larger than the moon"; "The sun is not larger than the moon"; and some about time: "Hippocrates lived at the time of the Peloponnesian War"; "Hippocrates did not live at the time of the Peloponnesian War"; and some about place: "The sun is second from the earth"; "The sun is not second from the earth"; and some about position: "The statue of Zeus at Olympia is seated"; "The statue of Zeus at Olympia is not seated"; and some about state: "The statue of Zeus is shod"; "The statue of Zeus is not shod"; and some about action: "Rose-water heats"; "Rose-water does not heat"; and some about passion: "We are naturally heated by rose-water"; "We are not naturally heated by rose-water."

2   Now, for clear and concise exposition, we call all premisses of this kind categorical, and following the custom of old, we call the parts they are composed of terms; for example, in "Dion is walking," "Dion" and "walking"; we take "Dion" as the subject term and "walking" as the predicate.

3   Whenever, then, the premiss is composed of a noun and a verb, the terms must be analyzed in this way; but when it is composed of nouns and a verb, as in "Dion is a man," we shall say that "Dion" is subject, "man" is predicate and that there is additionally predicated externally an auxiliary indicating the communion of the terms.

4   Now, whenever we predicate something of Dion, it is not possible to say either "all" or "some"; but whenever we make a predication of something else that can be divided, as of "man" or "tree," it is necessary to distinguish in the statement whether the predicate is asserted of all or some, and likewise if it is denied of all or some.

5   And so, let the premisses that are said with an "all" be called universally affirmative, as when we say, "Every man is an animal"; "Every sycamore is a tree"; and let the denials predicated of a whole class be termed negative or privative universally, as when we say, "No man is a *painting*; and let all that neither affirm nor deny of the whole class be called particular; for example, among particulars the affirmatives are of this sort: "Some man is an animal"; negatives of this sort: "Some man is not an animal"; an equivalent to the last premiss is the following: "Not every man is an animal"; this, too, we call a particular negative.

6   Whenever we predicate something of a substance that is defined not only according to species but also according to number, then it is no longer possible to say either "all" or "some" or "not all" or "none"; thus in "Dion is a man" none of the words mentioned can be added.

Chapter III

I   Another kind of premisses is of those by means of which we make assertion not about the being of things, but in the form, "if one thing is, another is," or, "if one thing is not, another is"; let such propositions be called "hypothetical"; one class of these, "the hypothetical by connection," whenever one says, "if some other thing is, necessarily this thing is"; the other class, the "separative," whenever, if one thing is not, another is, or, if one thing is, another is not.

2   For all Greeks, of the present or the past, saying "be" or "exist" implies no difference of meaning; and neither does "subsist"; for in modern usage this latter word, too, is used for the same conception; when we have memories of perceptible things, whenever we call them up in connection with motions, as of Athenians, let this action be called "thought," but when they are at rest, "conception"; there are also other such conceptions, not derived from memory of perceptions, but existing naturally in all men, and the ancient philosophers call them, when they are expressed in language, "axiom"; often, however, the Greeks call conception, "thought."

3   To return to the subject, whenever something is accepted as existing because something else exists, or (as we said "by connection"), the statement is called hypothetical by the ancient philosophers; and, by the same token [the statement is called hypothetical], whenever we understand that because one thing does not exist another does, e.g., "because it is not night, it is day"; but, to repeat, they call the latter statement "separative," although it is also called a "disjunctive axiom" by some of the newer philosophers; just as the former species of hypothetical premisses, which we said were named "by connection," is called "conditional"; the more fitting form of expression for the propositions, those, namely, which we said were called separative premisses, is that with the conjunction "or" (*êtoi*)—it makes no difference whether we say "or" in one syllable or two (i.e., *ê* or *êtoi*)— while for the conditionals, the more fitting form is that with "if" or "if haply" (*ei* or *eiper*), if haply these conjunctions have the same meaning.

4   So it is possible to name the following statement: "If it is day, the sun is above the earth," a conditional proposition, in the fashion of the newer philosophers, but in the fashion of the ancients, a hypothetical premiss by connection; but those of the following sort: "Either it is day or it is night," a disjunctive proposition with the newer, but a hypothetical by separation with the ancients.

5   The separative proposition is equivalent to this sort of statement: "If it is not day, it is night," which all those who attend to the words alone call a conditional, because it is expressed in the conditional form of speech, but those who attend to the nature of the facts call it disjunctive; likewise, in this form of speech: "If it is not night, it is day," is a disjunctive proposition by the very nature of the case, but it has in expression the form of a conditional.

Chapter IV

1   Now this state of affairs is a sign of complete conflict; but the other, as in, "If Dion is at Athens, he is not on the Isthmus," shows incomplete conflict.

2   For conflict has in common that the facts in conflict cannot exist together; it is differentiated, however, in that some conflicting facts, in addition to not existing together, cannot both be non-existent at the same time; while others can be in this state; whenever, therefore, they have only the property of not existing together, there is incomplete conflict, but whenever they have also the property of not being non-existent at the same time, there is complete conflict; for of facts of this kind it is necessary that one or the other do not exist.

3   Therefore, for the latter kind there is a double scheme of argument: (1) if the additional premiss that it is day be assumed, concluding that

it is not night; or again, (2) premissing that it is not day, concluding that it is night; but for incomplete conflict there is only one possibility, to premiss one of the things in conflict and thus to destroy the other (whatever premiss is so assumed, is with good reason called an "assumption").

4   Now in the case of incomplete conflict, it is customary for the Greeks to speak in the following way: "Dion is not both at Athens and on the Isthmus," and all sets of facts that share in incomplete conflict will be signified by an expression of this form; but if facts which have neither consequence nor conflict with each other should be stated in paired clauses, we shall call such a sentence "conjunctive," as in the example, "Dion is walking and Theon is talking"; for these facts, having neither consequence nor conflict, are understood as in conjunction.

5   Wherefore also, whenever we deny them [i.e., conjunctions], we shall say that that statement is either a "negative conjunction" or "conjunctive"; for it makes no difference to our present purpose to say "negative conjunctive" or "negative conjunction," since your object in every form of expression is to show clearly to your audience whatever you have in mind.

6   But here too the school of Chrysippus, paying attention to verbal expression rather than to the facts, calls all sentences composed by means of the conjunctive particles, even if derived from things in conflict or consequence, "conjunctives"; using names carelessly in matters in which accuracy of expression is important, but in matters in which the words have no difference of meaning, legislating for themselves private meanings; they would not use names in this way if they wished to speak Greek and to be clear to their hearers.

7   As a matter of fact, it will make no difference if you use the term "consequent" as it has just been used, or the term "following" or "conjoint"; for all such terms are said by a transfer [metaphor] of names from what in daily life is called "tied together" or "conjoined"; this (sc. consequence) occurs in many ways, which it is the function of the theory of proof to investigate, just as conflict, too, occurs in many ways.

Chapter V

1   But now let us assign their names to these propositions: so then, for clear and concise exposition, nothing prevents our calling propositions with complete conflict "disjunctives," and those of incomplete conflict "quasi-disjunctives"; let there be no quibble over whether to say "quasi" or "like-disjunctives"; but in some propositions it is possible

for more than one or for all the members to be true, and necessary for one to be true; some call propositions of this sort "paradisjunctives," since the disjunctives have one member only true, whether they be composed of two simple propositions or of more than two.

2   For "Dion is walking" is one simple proposition, and so also, "Dion is sitting"; and "Dion is lying down" is one proposition, and so, too, "He is running," and "He is standing still," but out of all of them is made a disjunctive proposition, as follows: "Dion either is walking or is sitting or is lying down or is running or is standing still"; whenever a proposition is composed in this way any one member is in incomplete conflict with each of the other members, but taken all together they are in complete conflict with one another, since it is necessary that one of them must be true and the others not.

3   In the case of complete conflict two syllogisms can be constructed if we take as an additional premiss that one of the members is true, or on the contrary is not true, and infer that the second is not true when the first one is, or is true when the first is not; but for incomplete conflict there is but one additional premiss, that one of the members is true, and but one conclusion, that the remaining member is not true.

4   It is this way when the conflict consists of two members; when there are more than two conflicting members, in the case of complete conflict, we can, either asserting one member to be true, deny all the rest, or denying all the rest, assert the one member to be true; it is not possible, however, by denying the one, to allow the rest to be true, or, asserting the rest, to deny that the one is true; on the other hand, in the case of incomplete conflict, by asserting some one member, we can deny the remaining number, but we will have no other additional premiss suitable for producing a syllogism.

5   In the case of the proposition hypothetical by connection, which Chrysippus and his school call a conditional axiom, if we take the antecedent as an additional premiss, we shall get the consequent as a conclusion, and, if we take the contradictory of the consequent as an additional premiss, we shall get the contradictory of the antecedent as a conclusion; but note that neither by taking the consequent as an additional premiss nor the contradictory of the antecedent can we get a conclusion.

Chapter VI

1   We call one argument or one proposition a contradictory of another when there is complete conflict between them, and it is absolutely necessary that one of them be true and the other not.

2   For hypothetical propositions the one [of the pair of contradictories] has the negative particle attached to it; for categoricals, (1) where the word "all" is attached, we shall prefix the negative to this; (2) in "Socrates is walking" we shall prefix the negative to the predicate, so as to make the sentence read: "Socrates is not walking"; we shall not need to prefix a negative to the universal negative proposition, since we have the particular affirmative contradictory to it, and likewise the universal negative is contradictory to this kind of affirmative proposition.

3   All such propositions are called coterminous because they share terms with one another; they invert with one another by interchanging the verbal expression of their terms, whenever the subject becomes predicate and the predicate subject; but they convert when, together with such an interchange, they are true together, the universal negative with itself, and likewise the particular affirmative with the particular, while the remaining particular negative converts with no proposition.

4   In the hypothetical propositions, inversion occurs when the verbal expression of the terms [i.e., members] is interchanged, conversion with the members then being contradicted; for, "If it is day, it is light" is inverted to "If it is light, it is day," and is converted to "If it is not light, it is also not day."

5   Such then is conversion of propositions; syllogisms with two premisses are convertible with one another when one premiss is common and the second premiss of one of them is the contradictory of the conclusion of the other; of syllogisms having more than two premisses we shall say not simply "one premiss" but shall add to it "or more," making the whole statement read as follows: "an argument is the converse of an argument when, having one or more premisses common, the remaining premiss of the one is the contradictory of the conclusion of the other."

6   And the case is similar with the "modes" (logicians call the schemata of arguments by the name "mode"): for example, in the argument composed from a conditional and the antecedent, concluding the consequent, which Chrysippus calls the first indemonstrable, the following is the mode: "If the 1st, the 2nd; but the 1st; therefore the 2nd"; for that composed of a conditional and the contradictory of the consequent, inferring the contradictory of the antecedent, which Chrysippus also names the second indemonstrable, it is as follows: "If the 1st, the 2nd; but not the 2nd; therefore not the 1st"; just as for his third, which from a negative conjunctive and one of its members, gives the contradictory of the other member, the mode is as follows: "Not both the 1st and the 2nd; but the 1st; therefore, not the 2nd"; likewise also for the fourth in his listing, which from a disjunctive and one of its members, infers the contradictory of the remaining member,

the mode is as follows: "Either the 1st or the 2nd; but the 1st; therefore, not the 2nd"; and then for the fifth, which, from a disjunctive
and the contradictory of one of its members, infers the other member,
the mode is as follows: "Either the 1st or the 2nd; but not the 1st;
therefore, the 2nd"; and so then, just as premisses in converse relation
are true together, so it is a property of true arguments and modes to
be syllogistic, so that the converse to a syllogistic mode is itself
syllogistic also.

7   Now the way in which syllogisms are generated by hypothetical
propositions has been shown except for one mode, the paradisjunctive,
for which there is a double distinction of minor premisses; for, either,
assuming all but one of the members not to be true, we can affirm that
one, or, if one should assume the one member not to be true, the
majority would remain, and give a disjunctive conclusion.

Chapter VII

1   In syllogisms of this sort the major premisses determine the minor;
for, neither in the disjunctive do more than two additional premisses
occur nor in the conditional, while in the case of incomplete conflict
it is possible to make one additional assumption only; wherefore
Chrysippus and his followers call propositions of this sort not only
determinative but also "tropic," the whole syllogism being pegged
upon them as the timbers on the keel of a ship.

2   Moreover, some of the Peripatetics, as well as Boethos, call syllogisms
from determinative premisses not only indemonstrable, but also
primary; and they no longer allow all the indemonstrable syllogisms
from categorical premisses to be called primary; and yet, in another
sense, such syllogisms are prior to the hypotheticals, if at least it is
granted that the propositions of which they are composed are certainly
prior; for no one will doubt that the simple is prior to the composite.

3   But about such disputes it is not important whether you try to solve
them or to ignore them; for it is necessary to know both branches of
the syllogisms, and this is the useful thing, but to call one kind prior
to the other and to teach so, is as each man pleases; but it is not fitting
to ignore them.

4   Now, as we have seen, all the hypothetical syllogisms have their
minor premisses necessarily fixed, but the categoricals have not; for
he who says, "Every noble thing is choiceworthy," finds, to be sure,
that to produce a syllogism, he must carry either "noble" or "choiceworthy" into the second premiss, but not carry along the identical
premiss, and he is not required either to affirm or deny [but may do

either], or to carry over one member only, as in the hypothetical, but he may combine the repeated term with whatever else he wishes.

5 For, on the one hand, he can make a syllogism by adding this kind of premiss to the former, "Every choiceworthy thing is good"; for the syllogism will be: "Every noble thing is choiceworthy; every choice-worthy thing is good; therefore, every noble thing is good"; on the other hand it is possible for him to predicate universally anything else and construct a syllogism of these terms; so indeed, by making another term subject to one of those terms, e.g., "noble," it is possible to make a syllogism; for example, thus, "Justice is noble; the noble is choice-worthy; therefore, justice is choiceworthy."

6 Now, by adding the second premiss in this way to the first you will construe the term common to both premisses as subject in the one and predicate in the other; it is also possible so to combine the premisses that the common term is predicated of both the other terms, as it is in syllogisms of the following sort: "Every noble thing is choiceworthy; not every pleasure is choiceworthy; therefore not every pleasure is a noble thing"; or also thus, so as to predicate both terms of the common term, as in the following: "Every noble thing is choiceworthy; every noble thing is praiseworthy; therefore, some praiseworthy thing is choiceworthy."

7 Now the old philosophers called that the "first figure" of the categorical syllogism in which the common term was subject to one of the extremes and predicate of the other; "second" in which it is predicate of both extremes, and "third" in which it is subject.

8 "Choiceworthy" is predicated of "noble" in this sort of premiss: "The noble is choiceworthy"; and noble is its subject, a term of which it is natural for choiceworthy to be predicated; among them [i.e., the "old philosophers"] to affirm does not signify the same thing as to predicate; for he, also, who denies, predicates.

9 Let it accordingly be said, in regard to "The noble is not a thing to be avoided," that "noble" is subject, and "thing to be avoided" is predicated negatively of it, while in "The noble is to be avoided," "to be avoided" is predicated of it affirmatively; and, since custom has prevailed, they call both the aforesaid premisses categorical, and on their account the syllogisms categorical also; both, however, are not affirmative, but are as they have been oppositely defined.

Chapter VIII

1 Now, there being three figures in the categorical premisses, in each of them occur more than one syllogism, just as among the hypotheticals, some indemonstrable and primary and some requiring demonstration.

2   Among the hypothetical propositions, however, all the others previously mentioned are indemonstrable and primary except that one that assumes the contradictory of the consequent and affirms the contradictory of the antecedent.

3   In the case of the categoricals, there are four indemonstrables in the first figure; the first, inferring from two universal affirmative propositions a universal affirmative conclusion—it is obvious that the conclusion is a proposition so-called from its position in relation to the premisses— the second, the one inferring from a proposition universally negative toward the major term and one universally affirmative towards the minor, a universally negative conclusion; the third, one having a particular affirmative conclusion from a universally affirmative major and a particular affirmative minor; and last, one inferring from a universally negative and a particular affirmative, a particular negative conclusion; of the others, no one hereafter is indemonstrable or self-evident.

4   The syllogisms in the other figures are demonstrated from the aforesaid; in the second figure there are four syllogisms, and in the third, six.

Chapter IX

1   But the first syllogism in the second figure, having the premiss of the major term universally negative and the other universally affirmative, is reduced, by conversion of the major premiss, to the second syllogism in the first figure, drawing a universally negative conclusion.

2   Next in order to this is the one somehow equivalent to it, having a universally affirmative premiss of the major term and the second premiss universally negative, by conversion of two propositions, the universally negative premiss and the conclusion, which is itself universally negative, has its reduction to the forementioned second syllogism in the first figure, with a universally negative conclusion.

3   The third among them, from a universally negative and a particular affirmative concludes a particular negative, being reduced by some people, through conversion of the universal premiss, to the fourth syllogism in the first figure.

4   The remaining syllogism of those in the second figure, the fourth, from a universal affirmative and a particular negative concludes a particular negative, receiving its proof both by reduction to the impossible and by the method named by Aristotle "exposition."

5   Now reduction to an impossible—it is also called a showing of an impossible—is as follows: let the first be predicated of all the second,

and not of some of the third; I say that the conclusion follows that the second is not predicated of some of the third; suppose this is not the case, but if possible, on the contrary let the contradictory conclusion be drawn, that the second is predicated of all the third; but, in fact, the first was said of all the second; therefore, the first will have been shown predicated of all the third, which is absurd; therefore, the second is not predicated of all the third, but of some of it.

6   The method of exposition is the following: since the first is not predicated of some of the third, let that part of the third it is not predicated of be taken and let it be the fourth; therefore, the first is predicated of none of the fourth, but also it is predicated of all of the second; therefore, the second is predicated not at all of the fourth; but the fourth is some of the third; therefore, the second is not predicated of some of the third.

Chapter X

1   Of the syllogisms in the third figure, the first, formed of two universally affirmative premisses, has a particular affirmative conclusion, being reduced by conversion of the minor premiss to the third syllogism in the first figure.

2   The second, from a universally negative major premiss and the other a universally affirmative, has a particular negative conclusion, having a reduction to the fourth syllogism in the first figure by conversion of the minor premiss.

3   The third, from a particular affirmative and a universal affirmative, has a particular affirmative conclusion, being reduced to the third syllogism in the first figure through conversion of the particular premiss and also of the conclusion.

4   The fourth, from a universal affirmative and a particular affirmative, signifies a particular affirmative, the minor premiss being converted.

5   The fifth, from a universal negative and a particular affirmative, has a reduction to the fourth syllogism in the first figure by converting the particular, making a particular negative conclusion.

6   The remaining sixth syllogism, from a particular negative and a universal affirmative, concludes a particular negative, being demonstrated through reduction to an impossible and through exposition, in the way shown in the case of the fourth syllogism of the second figure.

7   Through reduction to an impossible thus: let the first be denied of some of the third; and let the second be predicated of all the third: I say that the first will not be predicated of some of the second; for

suppose this is not true, but, if it be possible, let it be predicated of all; but the second was also predicated of all the third; consequently, the first will also be predicated of all the third; but by hypothesis it was not predicated of some; therefore, it will not be predicated of all the second; therefore, it will be denied of some.

8   The same thing can be shown through exposition, in this way: since the first is not predicated of some of the third, let that of which it is not predicated be taken and let it be the fourth; therefore, the first will be said of none of the fourth; but since the fourth is some of the third, the third will have been predicated of all of it; but also, the second is predicated of all the third, consequently it will also have been predicated of all the fourth; but also the first is predicated of none of the fourth; therefore, the first will not be predicated of some of the second.

Chapter XI

1   All the other combinations of premises in each of the figures are invalid and no syllogism arises from them because nothing is concluded necessarily, either dialectically or through demonstration; for men call "indication" the discovery of the truth about the thing in question arising out of the nature of the thing and made through following out the clues given by what is clearly observable; but an argument reaching a conclusion through true premises they call "demonstration."

2   In each figure there occur sixteen couplings of premises, because there are four types of premiss in each, two universal and two particular; they are apparently more numerous because of different forms of expression; one should train himself in those and recognize them, as has been set forth in my writing *On the Equivalent Propositions*; for the present work is an outline of logical study, not a detailed manual of instruction.

3   With the fourteen defined syllogisms, each having its proper conclusion, certain other propositions also coincide in truth, some of these being contained in the conclusions, others of necessity coinciding in truth with them; the corresponding particular propositions are contained in the universal conclusions, and with the universal affirmative propositions as conclusions other particulars follow by conversion and coincide in truth.

4   And for this reason, in the syllogisms of the first figure, having universal conclusions, namely, the first and the second, to the first the particular affirmative, to the second the particular negative [. . .].

5   And as a matter of fact, for some of the invalid couplings, though a conclusion does not follow straightway, as for the mentioned fourteen

that produce syllogisms, nevertheless, a conclusion does follow when the premisses are converted.

6   To be specific, in the first figure, if the premiss with the major term is affirmative, whether particular or universal, and the premiss with the minor is a universally negative proposition, there is no direct syllogism of the major term to the minor, but upon the premisses being converted a valid conclusion occurs, showing the minor predicated of the major, in the manner of the fourth syllogism in the same figure.

7   In the second and third figures nothing of this sort occurs by conversion of premisses; it does, however, occur in the third figure, in the third syllogism only, from the conversion of the conclusion; for the first two syllogisms of the second figure are converse to one another in the conclusion; and also the third and fourth in the third figure; and furthermore, just as in the first two syllogisms of the first and second figures the particular conclusions are embraced in the universal, so is it in the syllogisms in this figure.

Chapter XII

1   These syllogisms are called categorical, as I have said, and it is not possible to construct them in more than the three mentioned figures or in any other number in each figure; for this has been shown in my treatise *On Demonstration*; and we use them in the demonstrations in which there is a question about the magnitude of one of the things that exist, or what sort it is, or where it is situated or some similar question about things under the other categories.

2   For in investigating whether Eratosthenes correctly showed the greatest circle in the earth to measure 252,000 stades, the question is about the size of the circle, or its magnitude, or its quantity, or however you wish to name it, as also whenever one questions how many stades is either of the tropics on the earth, and, in each of the inhabited zones how large is the circle called Artic and the one called Antarctic, and for each zone how many degrees it is from the north.

3   The astronomers have sought for and demonstrated the magnitude of both the sun and the moon and of their distances, as also the magnitude of eclipses, whenever they are not total, but are a half or a third or some other fraction of the eclipsed bodies; and moreover the magnitude of the days in each of the inhabited zones has been sought and discovered, just as the other questions mentioned.

4   For it is common knowledge that, on the one hand, the magnitude of each day in the whole year has been discovered by the agency of clepsydras and water clocks, and sundials also and, on the other hand,

by the predictions of eclipses the size of sun and star and earth and how distant they are from our region, and such questions have been solved; and, in sum, whatever the methods are that investigate and prove the size of each of the things mentioned they use for the most part the categorical syllogisms of the first figure; for indeed all the enunciations about each of their investigations can be found demonstrated by them in universal terms.

5   And since these propositions can be in more or less general form, and some one of them, in relation to its most general class, seems to be stated particularly, for this reason, in such a case, some propositions and proofs appear particular; thus in relation to the proposition and proof about every triangle, that it has its three angles equal to two right angles, a proposition saying, not that every triangle, but that some, have their base angles equal to each other, would seem to be said particularly.

6   Now, stated thus, its enunciation and proof is not definite and scientific, but in the following way it is both scientific and universal: "Every isosceles triangle has its base angles equal to each other."

7   Both the expression indicating universality by prefixing numbers and the form without these is customary among the Greeks: for it is equally meaningful to say "Every isosceles triangle has its base angles equal to each other," and "The isosceles triangles have their base angles equal to each other."

8   And actually it is also a custom for the Greeks to express such statements in the singular number, and there is no difference in meaning if they say "All isosceles triangles have their base angles equal," or, "The isosceles triangle"; for looking at the species that belongs to all the particular, they rightly make the enunciation as if about one thing; for as species, it is one.

9   I say, "as species," since with respect to existence they are as many in number as there are particular bodies; but of such a species itself there is a single nature at which men look and say, e.g., that the weevil is a destructive animal, or the eagle feathered, or the bear savage.

Chapter XIII

1   Accordingly, the first syllogism of the first figure is the most appropriate to scientific demonstrations, being expressed by the Greeks in two forms, sometimes, as we have just said, "Man is an animal, animal is a substance, man is a substance"; and sometimes with "every": "Every man is an animal, every animal is a substance, every man is a substance."

2 Next in value is the second of the first figure, and in the second figure the first two sometimes become useful for demonstrations, since the universal affirmative is mingled in them.

3 And indeed, the third syllogism of the first figure, as was said a little before this, sometimes becomes useful for proofs, as when a triangle is isosceles, and further—for it has been shown—also the isosceles triangle has its base angles equal, from these facts it can be concluded that some triangle has its base angles equal.

4 There are some syllogisms in the third figure, as has been said before, that demonstrate the particular affirmative; and a particular negative is at times demonstrated in the three figures, as: "Every good thing is choiceworthy, the pleasure of the ignoble is not choiceworthy; therefore, the pleasure of the ignoble is not good."

5 Now in this expression pleasure specifically defined has been taken for the demonstration; in the following type it is more indefinite: "Every good is choiceworthy; some pleasure is not choiceworthy; therefore, some pleasure is not good"; in the following form of expression, also, a more indefinite statement occurs: "Every good is choiceworthy; not every pleasure is choiceworthy; therefore, not every pleasure is good."

6 It is clear that in a demonstration of this sort it is not magnitude, as in the aforementioned cases, but the quality of the thing that is demonstrated; for what sort of thing pleasure is, whether good, bad, or intermediate, is considered under the genus of quality; just as the equality of the base angles of an isosceles triangle is studied under relation.

7 He who shows that the earth is arranged at the center of the universe makes his study in the category of "where situated," just as he who shows that Hippocrates and Democritus did not live at the same time makes his demonstration in the category of "when they were born."

8 The one, however, who studies whether the earth is spherical makes his demonstration in the category of quality, as to express it differently, he who asserts that it is spherical has asserted a quality of the earth.

9 The questions of causes occur in the categories of action and passion; in medicine, e.g., from what causes come voice and breathing and nourishment and digestion; in philosophy, e.g., earthquake, thunderbolt, lightning, and thunder.

10 In the category of state the type of question is, who is the rich man, who is the poor man, who is the well-off, who is the beggar?

11 He who investigates how one weaves a cloak or plaits a net or makes a box or a bed, investigates "composition," a category passed over by Aristotle in his study of the ten categories, as I have shown in my commentary on that book.

12 There is another kind of category which Aristotle himself called

"position," that is, lying or sitting; for in "position" he says that those
things are said which indicate the postures of the parts of the body that
come about by their spatial relations to each other; and under this
category are Hippocrates's studies of what posture is best for a broken
leg or hand and for each of the other parts, and likewise the best
posture for the patient while the surgeon is treating collapses or
staunching hemorrhages or doing anything else of this sort.

Chapter XIV

1   What is most important and primary in regard to anything that is not
apparent to perception is the question of its existence or being; in this
respect the following kind of problems arise: "Does Fate exist?," "Is
there Providence?," "Do the gods exist?," "Is there a void?"

2   In these problems we use the hypothetical propositions, which the
ancients divided into those by connection and those by separation; the
Stoics call the connectives conditional axioms, the separatives, disjunctive, and we agree with them at least that there are two syllogisms
of the conditional axiom and two of the disjunctive.

3   But that there is not even one syllogism useful for demonstration
constructed from a negative conjunctive, as also that there is not a sixth
or 7th or 8th or 9th or other syllogism (in their sense of the term), has
been demonstrated elsewhere; but for the present it is proposed to list
only the useful ones, omitting the refutation of those superfluously
set up.

4   Chrysippus's school, believing there is a third indemonstrable
syllogism concluding from a negative conjunctive and one of its
members the contradictory of the remaining member, as in the following
example: "Dion is not both at Athens and on the Isthmus" [. . .] to
be useful for many demonstrations in all departments of daily life,
even including the law courts.

5   Since some of the facts and statements that conflict with one another
have their conflict whole and complete, being able neither to exist or
be true together, nor be non-existent or false together, while some have
a halfway conflict, not being able to be true together, but being able
to be false together, for this reason I have thought it right to call the
complete conflict by the name "disjunctive" and incomplete by the
name "conflict" simply, or, with an added adjective, "incomplete
conflict."

6   Under these conditions the said syllogism is useful, using the same
form of expression Chrysippus does, but not, however, being grounded
on the conjunctive, but on the conflicting things; for him many
differences are collected under the one form of the conjunctive.

7   For since there are three different relations between facts, one,
conflict, of things that never occur together, the second, consequence,
of things that always occur together, and third, things that sometimes
occur together and sometimes do not, all those facts that have neither
necessary consequence nor conflict give material for the conjunctive
proposition; e.g., "Dion is walking and Theon is talking"; it is clear
that the negation of this will be: "It is not the case both that Dion is
walking and Theon is talking."

8   The additional assumption is, "But in fact Dion is walking," or
"But Theon is talking," and the conclusion in the case of the first
assumption "Therefore, Theon is not talking," in the second case,
"Therefore Dion is not walking"; such material has been shown to be
absolutely useless for demonstration.

9   This matter has been discussed for the sake of clarity, at greater
length, perhaps, than necessary in view of our purpose of brevity, but
let us return to the subject, as if none of these side remarks had been
made.

10 The syllogisms that arise from hypothetical propositions are brought
to completion by a progression from one thing to another through
consequence or conflict, either complete or incomplete; and besides
these there is no third kind of progression from one thing to another
that is useful for demonstration.

11 There will be two syllogisms deriving from complete consequence,
and another two from complete conflict, and let those from consequence
be called first and second, and those from conflict, fourth and fifth,
since Chrysippus put it so; but the third, in expression the same as
Chrysippus's, but according to the nature of the things postulated, is
not the same; for its genesis is not, as he thought, from a negative
conjunctive, but from deficient conflict, and it has one affirmative,
additional assumption, not two, as does either of those kinds derived
from complete consequence and complete conflict.

Chapter XV

1   Since, as we have shown, there is deficient consequence expressed
in the propositions called paradisjunctives, these, too, will give rise to
two syllogisms; first: "The distribution of nourishment from the belly
to the whole body occurs, either by the food being carried along of its
own motion, or by being digested by the stomach, or by being attracted
by the parts of the body, or by being conducted by the veins."

2   (Let it be granted that all these actions could occur together; for in
fact, this is possible, and the paradisjunctive differed from the disjunctive in just this respect; in the latter, one member always was true

and none of the others, but in the former, one member always is true, but one of the others, or even all of those comprehended, may be true at the same time.)

3   These propositions have two possible additional assumptions: an outright denial of one or two only of the members; denying one, for example: "Distribution of nourishment from the belly into the whole body occurs either by the belly squeezing, or by the veins conducting, or by the parts attracting, or by the nourishment moving under its own power; but in fact the stomach does not squeeze; therefore, the nourishment is carried either by the veins conducting it, or by the parts attracting, or by its own power."

4   Obviously this conclusion will be a paradisjunctive also, of three members, as it would, too, if another member had been denied, as "the stomach squeezing" was in this example; for the remaining three make the conclusion one composed in the manner of a paradisjunctive proposition.

5   A second form of additional assumption will be one by which we shall say, "Neither does the belly send the nourishment, nor the veins conduct it, nor is it moved by itself," or we can premiss the denial in another combination of any three member propositions; for it can be done in many ways.

6   And if three are not the case, the fourth remains to be concluded, affirmatively and definitely; for as long as only one or two of the four are taken, the conclusion is a paradisjunctive.

7   This kind of syllogism will seem to admit of being the same as the following: "If nourishment is distributed from the belly to the whole body, either it undergoes this through self-motion or by being sent by the stomach, or by being attracted by the parts, or conducted by the veins"; but it is not the same.

8   But the latter has the same force as the first indemonstrable syllogism of the hypotheticals, the distribution of nourishment being by hypothesis antecedent, and what was said next following as consequent, and it makes no difference whether the inferred conclusion is, in respect to its material, disjunctive or paradisjunctive; for the force of the first indemonstrable is consistent with either of the forms, since it is as follows: "If the first, either the second or the third or the fourth or the fifth"; then the minor premiss, "but the first; therefore, either the 2nd or the 3rd or the 4th or the 5th"; a second minor premiss, in the manner of the second of the indemonstrables is the following: "But neither the 2nd nor the 3rd nor the 4th nor the 5th; therefore, not the 1st."

9   The syllogism I spoke of a little earlier is constructed on the paradisjunctive major, when the facts are admittedly to be construed paradisjunctively, and it takes a minor premiss as if it were a disjunctive,

as in the following case: "Nourishment is either distributed by itself, or it was sent by the stomach, or it is conducted by the veins, or it is attracted by the parts of the body"; the syllogisms in the disjunctive mode have two minors, that is, either one member exists, or all but one do not.

10 That syllogisms of this sort are useful for demonstration Plato, also, shows in the *Alcibiades*, having made use, in effect, of the second of the hypotheticals, where he says, "If Alcibiades knows justice, he either learned it from another or knows it by having discovered it himself"; then, having shown that he neither had learned it from another nor had discovered it himself, he draws the conclusion that Alcibiades does not know justice.

11 By the simple paradisjunctive the question would have been treated in the following way: "Alcibiades knows justice either by having learned it or by having discovered it himself; but he does not know it through having learned it; therefore, he knows it through having himself discovered it."

Chapter XVI

1 There is also another species of syllogisms, a third, which I call relational, but the disciples of Aristotle try to force them into the number of the categorical syllogisms; they are of no little use to "skeptics" and arithmeticians and calculators, in arguments such as these: "Theon has twice as much as Dion, but Philon in turn has twice as much as Theon; therefore, Philon possesses four times as much as Dion."

2 And stated conversely the argument, the same in effect, will proceed in this way: "Dion possesses half as much as Theon; but Theon has half as much as Philon; therefore, Dion possesses a fourth part of the amount of Philon's property."

3 A syllogism will proceed demonstratively in this way also concerning any other multiple ratio; for if a given number should be triple another, and again, another triple that triple, the greatest number would be nine times the least, and conversely, the least will be the ninth part of the greatest.

4 So also in addition and subtraction; for if a first number is equal to a second, and another equal number is added to each, the sum of one addition will be equal to the other sum, and if equals are subtracted from each of two equals, the remainder of the one will also be equal to the other remainder.

5 As I have said, there is a great number of such syllogisms, both in arithmetic and in reckoning, all having in common the fact that they

have the cause of their structure derived from certain axioms; keeping these axioms in mind in connection with the given arguments, we shall be able to begin again more clearly and reduce such syllogisms to the categorical form.

6   For since there is this self-evident axiom, "Things equal to the same thing are also equal to one another," it is possible to reason and demonstrate as Euclid made his demonstration in his first theorem showing that the sides of the triangle are equal; for since things equal to the same thing are also equal to one another, and the first and second have been shown equal to the third, the first would thus be equal to each of them.

7   Again, since there is this self-evident axiom, "If equals be added to equals the sums are also equal," if, assuming the first and second equal to each other, an equal be added to each of the equals, one sum will also be equal to the other sum, and we can state it thus: "Since the first is equal to the second, and the 3rd is added to the first and the 4th to the second, these also being equals, the one sum will be equal to the other."

8   In like manner, whenever equals are subtracted from any equals, we shall be able to say, "Since the sum is equal to the sum, and from each of them these equals are subtracted, the one remainder is also equal to the other remainder."

9   So also, the double of the double will be quadruple; that is, if a double be taken of something else, and again the double of it be taken, the 3rd will be quadruple the 1st.

10   Similarly, in all other cases the structure of the demonstrative syllogism will be by virtue of a conjoined axiom, both for numbers and for other things that themselves belong also to the category of relation; for also in these cases the syllogism will depend on one of the axioms, e.g., "If Sophroniscus is the father of Socrates, Socrates is the son of Sophroniscus," and conversely, "If Socrates is the son of Sophroniscus, Sophroniscus is the father of Socrates."

11   The minor premisses to the propositions stated are obvious; this syllogism will proceed hypothetically thus: "If Socrates is the son of Sophroniscus, Sophroniscus is the father of Socrates; but Socrates is the son of Sophroniscus; therefore, Sophroniscus is the father of Socrates"; the structure of the reasoning will be more forced in categorical propositions; clearly, in this case too, a certain general axiom being premissed, to wit: "The man whom someone has as father, of him he is the son; Lamprocles has Socrates as father; therefore, Lamprocles is the son of Socrates."

12   Similarly, syllogisms used in the discussion of any form of relation will get the credibility of their structure and their demonstrative force by means of a general axiom; as for example, those arguments involving

"the more," since it is clear that these too are of the same kind as those constructed in the category of relation; examples of these have been given (using the word "more") in the commentaries about these arguments; the following kind of syllogism is expressed without the word "more" but with its force, e.g., "The virtue of the better is worthier of choice; soul is better than body; therefore, the virtue of the soul is worthier of choice than the virtue of the body."

13 Similar to these is this kind of syllogism: "The good of the better is worthier of choice; soul is better than body; therefore, that of the soul is worthier of choice than that of the body."

Chapter XVII

1 Nearly all the syllogisms get their structure through the cogency of the universal axioms that are set over them; since it was only later that I understood this, it is not written either in my commentaries *On Demonstration* or in *On the Number of the Syllogisms*.

2 And yet we knew relational syllogisms even at the time of those studies, having discovered the manner of their structure and validity; but that all demonstrative syllogisms are such through the cogency of universal axioms can be learned more clearly by all those who have examined such arguments in whatever way they have been worked out; for instance: "You say, 'It is day'; but you are also telling the truth; therefore, it is day."

3 Such a syllogism, too, is demonstrative, because the universal axiom it falls under is true, being as follows: "What a man who tells the truth says is so; someone, say Theon, says, 'It is day,' and Theon always tells the truth; therefore, it is day"; this is also said more clearly thus: [. . .] "therefore it is day."

4 For he who says that this thing is says the same as one who says that there is something among existing things and that this thing is, just as he who says that this thing exists says the same as he who says this is; and, moreover, he who says, "It is true that it is day," says the same as he who says, "It is day."

5 And for this reason you must be trained in exercises on equivalent propositions; at times it is possible to discern propositions that are different from each other but say in effect the same thing, while in other cases they do not say the same thing but obviously have opposite meanings, as for example, if something, on the one hand bears fruit and another having long [. . .].

6 The question of meanings often intrudes into a discussion of this sort; some claiming that the word signifies many meanings and needs

distinguishing marks of its different senses, and not a few failing completely to note what is often signified by it, though that is most clear and known to all Greeks, as we have shown in the case of the word "to tell the truth"; for all the Greeks say that he tells the truth who reveals things that are or were, as they are or were, just as he tells a lie who says that things that are not are, or that things that are, are not.

7   One who is reasoning and demonstrating must pay heed to two primary and important points: (1) to hear what is signified by the word according to the custom of the Greeks; and (2) to note whether the premiss assumed carries conviction as falling under a universal axiom and through that very fact, or through some other reason—for most of the things men reason about and demonstrate are said by force of an axiom—keeping in our minds also the meaning of the word axiom; for we laid it down that in the present exposition we give this name to a proposition that is self-evident.

8   This kind of argument is often involved with the meaning of a word, as indeed, in the very argument just mentioned, which I called the one through the thing defined, one might more clearly argue as follows: "Truth is a statement expressing existing things; Dion always speaks the truth; but he says that there is such a thing as divination; therefore, there is such a thing as divination; for if Dion always speaks the truth, obviously he speaks this thing truly, that divination exists; if that divination exists is true, divination exists."

9   For in this argument, that "A proposition expressive of existing things" is signified by the word truth, is an explanation of what is meant by the word "truth," and the statement that Dion always tells the truth has been substituted for the universal axiom, but the conclusion is the following: "If Dion always tells the truth, and one of the things he says is that divination exists, this, too, is true."

Chapter XVIII

1   About this topic what has been said will suffice for the present, but let us pass on to another point, to wit: since, as there are relational syllogisms dealing with "more and less," so there are those dealing with "likewise" or proportion, we must examine whether the validity of the latter, too, is derived from universal axioms; let it make no difference whether we say "likewise" or "equally" or "similarly."

2   This type of argument is that of Plato as written in the *Republic*; for Socrates maintains that as a city becomes just and is called so, so also does a soul become just and so-called, likewise, both action and law, and anything whatever of the things called just, are so called according to the same meaning.

3   For the Idea of justice, from which all particular just things receive
their name, is the same in all; but if there is one same thing, to whatever
one of the particulars it may be clearly attributed, from this it can also
be transferred to the others, since we know that the same Idea does not
appear with equal clarity in all cases, but in some cases it appears more
clearly, in others more confusedly.

4   And for this reason, having first exercised the young men who share
the conversation with him in a discussion about the just city, he then
passes over to the soul and demonstrates that this, too, is called just in
the same way as the city, so as to make the following syllogism: "In
like manner are city and soul called just and are just; a city is said to be
just through each of its parts doing its own business; a soul, therefore,
will be called just, too, by this principle."

5   Since many things are demonstrated by arithmeticians and geometers
in the same form of argument, and it can be clearly and naturally
apparent to all men that whatever is so demonstrated is convincing, I
have, for this reason, written about this syllogism also in my study of
the syllogisms; for those inexpert in arithmetic and geometry let the
following be a paradigm of the concept: "As the 1st is to the 2nd, so
also the 3rd to the 4th."

6   In arguments of this sort everyone understands and believes the
following general axiom: "Things which are in general in the same
ratio, are also in the same particular ratio"; and so he who posits that
the 1st is in the same ratio to the 2nd as the 3rd to the 4th, and that the
ratio of the 1st to the 2nd is the double, will not deny that the ratio of
the 3rd to the 4th is double, just as if the ratio of the 1st to the 2nd is
the triple, he will say that that of the 3rd to the 4th is triple also, or if
quadruple or fivefold or however he reckons the 1st to the 2nd, it will
be apparent that the 3rd to the 4th is also quadruple or fivefold.

7   For if, in the universal, the same ratio holds between the first and
the 2nd as between the 3rd and the 4th, there will also be the same ratio
in the particular ratios; and one of the particular ratios is the fivefold;
therefore, this is the ratio of the 3rd to the 4th.

8   All these syllogisms, indeed, must be said to belong, first to the
genus of relational syllogisms, but secondly, in species they are constructed according to the force of an axiom; as Posidonius also says
they are called "conclusive by force of axiom."

Chapter XIX

1   Since the members of the Peripatetic school have written about the
syllogisms called "by added assumption" as useful, (but they seem to

me to be superfluous, as I have shown in my treatise *On Demonstration*), it would seem proper to say something about them.

2   How many and what they are, it is not necessary to detail completely here, since I have spoken about them in those commentaries; but what sort of thing their species is, will be said here in two examples.

3   One kind is of this sort: "Of what this is predicated, this too is predicated; but this of this; therefore, this also of this"; or in names: "Of what tree, also plant; but tree of sycamore; therefore, plant of sycamore"; obviously, one must understand in addition to what is put in words the verb "is predicated" or "is said of," so as to make the complete expression, "Of what tree is predicated, plant is predicated; but tree is predicated of sycamore; therefore, plant will be predicated of sycamore."

4   Another kind of syllogism by added assumption is, "What of this, of this also; but this of this; therefore, also of this"; in words: "What of tree, of sycamore; but plant of tree; therefore, plant of sycamore."

5   That such syllogisms are compends of categoricals, not another kind of them, has been shown in the commentaries mentioned above and I need speak no more of them here; for in introductory treatments of syllogisms none of the useful ones should be omitted, but it is not necessary to give refutations of the superfluous ones.

6   For this reason, then, I need not show that the syllogisms constructed by Chrysippus in his three books of *Syllogistics* are useless: for I have shown this elsewhere, as well as concerning the ones he calls "perantic"; for some of these were shown not to be a special kind of syllogism, but syllogisms expressed in a tortured form of speech, at times by transposition of consequence [. . .] but those called subsyllogistic being stated in expressions equivalent to the syllogistic; superfluous, moreover, are those, finally, that they call "unmethodical," by which one must reason when there is no orderly argument at all.

Commentary

Section 1

The first sentence of the section is mutilated by the obliteration of a few words in the MS. Kalbfleisch conjectures and prints as the beginning of the sentence the words: *tôn phainomenôn ta men aisthései gigno—*. He supports his conjecture by reference to two passages in *De Temperamentis* (Kuehn, I, 587, 590) and two in *De Methodo Medendi* (Kuehn, X, 36, 38). In these passages the two kinds of immediate knowledge, sense perception and intellectual intuition (*noêsis*), are asserted. In the first passage of the *De Methodo Medendi* the usage of the "old philosophers" in setting up two classes of *phainomena*, those discerned by sense and those falling under intellectual intuition by "a first indemonstrable apprehension," is explicitly distinguished from the view of the empirics, who recognize sense alone. Therefore, there is Galenic authority for the conjecture of the word *phainomenon* in this place, and for the doctrine of the clause.

That this way of knowing is a universal human attribute is emphasized in the words, *gignôskomen hapantes anthropoi*. There may be a conscious echo of the first sentence of Aristotle's *Metaphysics*. Since the doctrine of the first chapter is derived from Aristotle, this would not seem unlikely. At any rate, Galen's interest in logic is directed toward its usefulness for demonstration rather than toward the theoretical question of the reasons for the validity of logical forms. Validity of the valid forms he takes for granted. His criterion is what forms are useful for demonstration. Thus the first chapter remarks on the place of demonstration in relation to the acquisition of knowledge, before the analysis of the forms of reasoning is taken up.

The teaching that sense perception and intellectual intuition each give a kind of immediate knowledge, the one of universal concepts, the other of the principles of demonstration, is contained in the last chapter of the *Posterior Analytics*, as Ernst Kapp (*Greek Foundations of Traditional*

Logic) has pointed out. The use of *phainomena* as a term covering both objects of sense and objects of intellect seems strange to a modern ear. We are accustomed to "phenomena" meaning appearances. Galen's term means anything which might be the subject of *phainetai*. That the usage has support in Aristotelian terminology is seen in the statement in *de Motu Animalium* (702 a 19) that *phantasia* occurs either through intellectual intuition (Galen's word *noêsis*) or through sense perception. It is true that in *de Anima* (427 b) Aristotle defines *phantasia* in close connection with *aisthêsis*, yet he is, as the above quoted passage shows, not always exact in his use of the term. In the *de Anima* passage, the emphasis is on the psychological structure of the mind. In other passages the word may be used more loosely. Plato in *Theaetetus* (152 c) derives *phantasia* from *phainetai*, suggesting that he was introducing an unfamiliar word. Although in this passage he ties it in with *aisthêsis*, the context suggests that he considered it to have a broader extension than the latter term. Galen, in any case, finds the word *phainomena* acceptable as a term covering things directly apprehended without regard to the mode of apprehension. In this sentence Galen is not concerned with the psychological machinery of such apprehension, but with the common quality that both modes give immediate knowledge. Galen, of course, is not thinking of Plato's and Aristotle's use of *phainomenon* in the sense of "apparent but not necessarily true." Galen would probably say that when we know the *phainomena*, we know them through sense or intellectual intuition, regardless of times when our phantasia is mistaken.

Section 2

The first sentence of the *Posterior Analytics* clearly states the doctrine that demonstration proceeds from things already known to knowledge of a conclusion: *Pasa didaskalia kai pasa mathêsis dianoêtikê ek proüparchousês gnôseôs* (71 a 1f). The consequence of this doctrine presents Aristotle with the problem of whence comes this prior knowledge, which he attempts to solve in the last chapter (*Anal. Post.*, II), the doctrine of which Galen, as has been said, condenses into the preceding section of this chapter.

Galen condenses also Aristotle's teaching that the prior knowledge must be "proper" (*oikeion*) to what is to be demonstrated. Aristotle says (*Anal. Post.*, 71 b 20–25) that demonstrative knowledge must come from propositions that are "true, primary, immediate, and better known than the conclusion, prior to it and the cause of it; in this case the principles will be *oikeiai* to the proposition being demonstrated." He says (74 b 26) that not all true premises are proper. Galen seems to mean by proper something more general and more commonplace: that however true a proposition may be it will not lead to a desired conclusion if it is about something unrelated to that conclusion.   Aristotle expresses this thought by saying that each science has its appropriate principles.

Galen's fifteen books, *de Demonstratione*, unfortunately no longer extant, are testimony to his studious concern with demonstration. Undoubtedly, his controversial relations with fellow physicians stimulated his desire to master the correct methods of demonstration.   One must agree with I. von Mueller's judgment (*Beweis*, p. 28) that Galen's treatment of demonstration emphasizes the practical aspects of it in contrast to Aristotle's theoretical interest.   Many quotations from *de Demonstratione* in his extant works show this orientation of his thinking, and it is equally evident here and in later passages of the *Institutio*.   The phrase "useful for demonstration" or its opposite occurs several times as a criterion for the acceptability of logical forms.   He looks on logical forms more from the point of view of their effectiveness in establishing the truth of inferences than from the point of view of their logical validity. He makes little or no attempt to explain logical validity, but spends much time in showing how the different forms are appropriate to different subject matters.   The third clause of this section, "since indeed . . . we can persuade, etc." illustrates this approach.   It envisions demonstration as an argument in which the speaker is trying to convince a reluctant opponent by means of a logical demonstration.   This is the standpoint of the *Topics* rather than of the two *Analytics*.

In his commentary Mau considers this clause hopelessly corrupt and does not translate.   It should be remarked that the comment here presupposes Kalbfleisch's conjecture.

The clause just referred to is not as clearly expressed as it might be. In the first place it is somewhat uncertain whether it is meant to explain the necessity of starting from prior knowledge or from appropriate premises.   Then, the compulsion supposed would seem better placed in reference to the acceptance of the conclusion than to the premises. The Greek, however, seems to require the latter interpretation.

The example of demonstration which Galen gives is interesting in view of the latter chapters of the *Institutio*.   In Chapters XVI and the two following he returns to demonstrations of the sort instanced here, calling them relational syllogisms and remarking that they are much used in mathematical reasoning.   Whatever inspired Galen to the study of this kind of logic, he has introduced into his discussion a study that is not found so far as we know in previous treatments of logic.   While it is true that Aristotle, under the influence of the Academy, uses examples of mathematical arguments, they are presented from the point of view of his logic, as illustrative of the finding of middle terms, for instance, and not from the point of view of the mathematician himself.   Here and in the later chapters, Galen analyzes arguments involving relational terms, such as "equal," and seeks out the structure of reasoning that depends on the peculiar relational properties of such terms.   Thus, at the beginning of his work, Galen serves notice that the field of logic is broader than the area covered by the categorical and hypothetical syllogisms of the Peripatetic and Stoic traditions.

The names Dion, Philon, and Theon are the John Doe and Richard Roe of ancient philosophical exposition.   They seem to have originated with the Stoics or at least to have been given currency in their writings. (Philon occurs in Aristotle, *de Interp.*, 16 b 1.)   They meet us in Stoic contexts in Diogenes Laertius, Sextus Empiricus, and Alexander of Aphrodisias used in the same way that Aristotle uses letters of the alphabet to abstract the logical form of a proposition from its material reference.

Section 3

In this section Galen analyzes the example of a demonstration given in the preceding section, with an important difference.   Where before he deduced the equality of Theon to Dion from the two propositions asserting the equality of each to Philon and adds that the conclusion follows through the axiom, "things equal to the same thing, etc.," he now incorporates the axiom as one of the premises.   In Chapter XVI he returns to this twofold form of the argument and explains that the second way of handling it is due to the Peripatetics, who thereby assimilate the argument to the form of the categorical syllogism.   He remarks there that the Peripatetic method is "violent."   Mau rejects Kalbfleisch's *triôn* as the number of the parts of the syllogism on the ground that four are given.   I would defend *triôn* on the basis of *tritou* (line 4) and the following clause which puts the conclusion on a different footing.

Section 4

Since the introductory chapters of the *Institutio* are concerned with defining the terms of logic, Galen has to concern himself with the varia- tions in terminology that resulted from the different approaches of writers in the different schools, especially the Peripatetic and the Stoic, as these were the schools that originated most of the technical work in logic.   He uses *hoi palaioi* and *hoi neoteroi* to refer to these schools.   In this he conforms to the practice of Sextus and of Alexander.   Elsewhere in his writings the former term may refer generally to "the ancients," e.g., Plato or Hippocrates, and the latter may refer to the more recent writers of other schools (e.g., *hoi neoteroi tôn Akademaikôn*, Mueller, *Hipp. et Plat.*, p. 796).   In this work, however, the usual accompaniment of the former term is a known Peripatetic expression, and of the latter a Stoic, so that it is safe to conclude that they are terms for the two schools. It is of course possible, since the early Stoic logic was founded upon Aristotelian logic, that *hoi neoteroi* means more recent Stoics. Some of the terms attributed to them, however, are known to have been used, if not invented, by Chrysippus (see Appendix I).

The word *symperasma* is Aristotle's regular name for the conclusion of a syllogism. In the *Prior Analytics* (e.g., 32 a 8–14) Aristotle distinguishes carefully between *symperasma* and syllogism. However, Aristotle (30 a 16) does use the word syllogism for the conclusion of a syllogism. Since Aristotle himself was guilty of the mistake, Galen's warning to beginners was no doubt called for. The opposite extension of *symperasma* to the whole syllogism is an easy transition and must have become sanctified by usage. There is a certain heat in Galen's rejection of the former confusion that is unusual in this even-tempered book, and perhaps hints at some personal conflict with a rival logician.

Section 5

"Premiss" is Aristotle's word (*protasis*) for either of the premisses of the syllogism. In the preceding section "assumption" translates *lemma*, since Galen indicates its derivation from *lambano*. It seems to be a Stoic word for "premiss"; it does not occur in *Prior Analytics*, but does at least once in *Topics* (156 a 2). In defining "premiss" as a proposition embodying prior knowledge and set forth for a conclusion to be drawn from it, Galen seems to be differentiating it from the "assumption." Possibly there is an obscure reference to an interpretation of the difference between the categorical and hypothetical syllogisms, in that the former starts from something known, while in the latter, the hypothetical major may be known before the truth of its antecedent is discovered. If so, this distinction is never clearly stated in the remainder of the book.

"Axiom" (*axiôma*) is often used by Aristotle in the sense Galen gives it here. It is not the term Euclid uses for the axioms of geometry; they are called "common notions," which is a term in Stoic epistemology. But here and elsewhere Galen cites Euclid's common notions as examples of *axiômata*, though he also calls propositions such as "everything has a cause" axioms (Kuehn, X, 36). The definition given here is referred to in Chapter XVII, 7, in the discussion of syllogisms "conclusive by force of an axiom."

The last sentence refers to the Stoic use of "axiom" as a name for any proposition. Galen sometimes adopts that usage when he is discussing Stoic logic. His tolerant attitude to difference in terminology is characteristic of all Galen's writings and reflects his opposition to the pedantic formalism of the Stoics, which will meet us again.

CHAPTER II

Section I

The second chapter of the *Institutio* continues with the explanation of logical terms. It follows the traditional order of Aristotle's *Organon*, treating the subjects of terms and propositions in language derived from the *Categories*, the *de Interpretatione* and the first chapter of Book I of the *Prior Analytics*. There are, however, indications in the content of Stoic influence and of the interests of the second and first centuries B.C.

In this first section a list of propositions containing predicates from each of the ten Aristotelian categories is given, in both affirmative and negative form. In some cases, about half, the double form is emendation. Mau casts doubt on the complete carrying through of this parallelism. His reasons are that where the double form occurs in the MS. there was a real question at the time as to which statement, the affirmative or the negative, was true; where it does not occur the question was regarded as settled. The categories are called by their Aristotelian names, except that "magnitude" is substituted for "quantity." The ten categories are preceded by a pair of propositions, which Galen calls ones that affirm or deny simple existence. Mau, reading MS. *eiper* for Kalbfleisch's *eipes* makes a single hypothetical proposition out of this pair. They stand for Aristotle's "first substance," while the next examples illustrate "second substance." Nowhere, though, in the section are the classes of predicates called "categories." In Chapter XII, however, Galen does refer to them under that name. The interest of the section is not directed to the ontology of predicates but to their logical function as terms in premisses.

The examples chosen to illustrate the categories repay study for the clues they give to the source of Galen's material. The dependence on Aristotle for the list and order of the categories is complete. No mention is made of Galen's own claimed addition of a category of "composition," mentioned later (ch. XIII, 11). The propositions enunciated, however, have the flavor of the encyclopedic lore that was flourishing in the second and first centuries B.C. and have a certain Stoic cast. It is not so much that they deal with questions that were unknown to the immediate followers of Aristotle, but that they reflect the kind of interest that is catered to by handbooks of authoritative opinions rather than the direct concern of first rate minds formulating and studying the problems of nature. The device of giving the affirmative and negative of the same proposition is enlivened by the selection of statements about subjects that were a matter of dispute among scholars. For instance, the illustration of the category of quantity by the sentence, "The sun is a foot wide," certainly reflects the dispute between the Epicureans and other schools about the size of the sun. The Epicureans maintained that it was about the size that it appears to be, or a little larger or smaller. The interest in the question is reflected in the notice "Aëtius" (ps.- Galen, *History of Philosophy*, Kuehn, XIX, 276), gives to the subject. Here the opinions of the pre-Socratics, the Stoics, and the Epicureans are given. The sharp distinction between the latter two is brought out, as the Stoics are said to state that it was greater than the earth (likewise the moon), while the Epicureans held the opinion already stated. The example in the text is clearly an allusion to the opinion quoted by Aëtius from Heraclitus, that the sun was the width of a human foot.

In similar fashion, the statement that the sun is or is not second from the earth points to a difference of opinion noticed by Aëtius between Plato, who held so, and later astronomers, who placed it midway between the other planets. The question whether or not air is a "body" is similar; it further shows the kind of encyclopedic concern with all kinds of "scientific fact" that is displayed in this list. This interest extended to historical questions (the date of Hippocrates, possibly a contribution by Galen himself), to sightseeing (the statue of Zeus at Olympia), and to medicine (the medicinal properties of rose water, another contribution of Galen's ?).

The first pair of propositions are unique in that the affirmative and negative have different subjects. Providence exists, there is no centaur. Probably Galen or his source felt that it was impious, even for the purpose of illustrating a logical form, to deny the existence of Providence, while the denial of the existence of centaurs would offend no one. If Mau's quoted opinion is correct, this paragraph must be modified.

It is clear from the choice of examples that the compiler of the list wished to use those that were not obviously true or false, except in the case of the first pair, since logic is, as conceived here, fundamentally a science of obtaining knowledge. The substitution of a second subject for the negative of the first pair may have been to avoid a special difficulty entailed by propositions about first substance, which are essentially existential propositions. Since Aristotle's *ho tis anthrôpos* (*Cat.* 1 b 4) is not a name for a first substance but a general reference to the kind, a name must be used in an affirmative or negative sentence with a subject in first substance, having existence alone predicated of it. There would be no room for debate in asserting or denying the existence of a known singular substance; therefore he chose subjects, Providence and a centaur, about which debate was possible.

The use of the proposition about Providence is an indication of the Stoic cast of the material. The encyclopedic range of the list points toward the school, or at least the influence, of Posidonius. None of the examples suggest a later date than the time of Posidonius, unless the use of Hippocrates is Galen's own. In addition to the range, the kind of subjects—the astronomical, the chronological, and the tourist types—also point to the period when discussions between the schools were centered, in lively fashion, on the latest work in the sciences and on the increasing interest in the various parts of the world and on its past history.   Furthermore, the list, while tedious, as befits an introduction to logic, is intelligent and shows a firm grasp of the essential theory of the categories.   It belongs to the period when the form of the theory is fixed but not yet stereotyped.   Therefore, it is reasonable to conclude that it formed the part of a pedagogical handbook, composed for use in training pupils in philosophy who will be expected to think and not merely to memorize a frozen set of dogmas.

One further observation about the content of the list is in order.   The examples are examples of propositions and follow the paragraphs, at the end of the preceding chapter, in which the propositions (premisses and conclusion) that occur in a demonstration are named.   Two things are clear: in this second chapter the analysis of demonstration is carried out as far as the analysis of the simple sentences that occur in categorical syllogisms, sentences in which a single predication is made of a single subject; secondly, the metaphysical or ontological aspect of the categories is not brought into prominence, for the analysis is purely grammatical and logical; it is grammatical in exhibiting the structure of simple predication in affirmation and denial, and logical in so far as the list of propositions follows the Aristotelian classification of the kinds of predicates.   There is, however, no discussion of substance, property, and accident, or of absolute and relative terms, or of genera and species, or of any of the questions about the kind of being that the different classes of predicates possess or how they are related to one another.

One particular characteristic of the list is related to this latter distinction. The subjects of the propositions given as examples are all singulars.   No doubt this is partly a result of the method being followed.   The definition of propositions with universal subjects, taken totally or partially, has not yet been introduced.   It has, however, the advantage of a kind of generality.   Since Galen is going to treat of hypothetical syllogisms as well as categorical, and since hypothetical syllogisms frequently are composed of propositions having singular subjects, this discussion can serve as an introduction to both kinds of syllogisms.   Lastly, the kind of encyclopedic information that was drawn on in the composition of the list offered mainly singular propositions of the sort we have been examining.

Finally, a word about the text of the section is required.   Since the categories are exhibited in pairs of affirmative and negative propositions, it is obvious that the text offered a field day to the haplographer. Kalbfleisch has filled in the words that have thus been omitted, with as near to absolute certainty as can be obtained in this kind of textual restoration.   In one case, this was done with the category of state (*echein*);

the name of the category itself had dropped out and is restored by Kalbfleisch, thus incidentally disposing of Prantl's argument against the authenticity of the work on the ground that the list of categories, by omitting "state" did not correspond to Aristotle's list, and so could not have been incorporated by Galen, who knew Aristotle very well.

Sections 2 and 3

The term "categorical," as applied to simple propositions, is not found in *Prior Analytics*. It was needed only after the development of the theory of hypothetical syllogisms made it necessary to distinguish the types of propositions that made up the different kinds of syllogisms. The adjective is derived from *katêgoreô*, which Aristotle (*Cat.*, 2 a 21 *et alibi*) uses to mean "to predicate of." He uses the adjective occasionally in the sense of "affirmative" proposition. The meaning "categorical" is found in Stoic sources, for obvious reasons. Mau suggests Galen's use of the first person of the verb for name and that he speaks of "terms" (*horos*) according to the old custom means that Galen is here introducing the term categorical in its later traditional sense.

The analysis of the proposition into "terms" is found in Aristotle, both in *de Interpretatione* and in *Prior Analytics*, and the word *horos* is Aristotle's. It is apparently in origin an arithmetical term, used for the "terms" in a proportion. The distinction between a predication made by a verb and one made by a copula and predicate noun is familiar to Aristotle, but the analysis here, with the use of the word *epirrhema*, is more grammatically precise, though it does not stress the point made by Aristotle, that a verbal predication may be analyzed into a copula and participle. *Epirrhema* is a technical term of the formalized grammar of Alexandrian times and usually means "adverb." The more general sense of "auxiliary," which it has here, may reflect an earlier usage. If so, the scrap of doctrine stated in this section may be traceable to the old Stoics. The use of the type name "Dion" points to Stoic sources. The terms *"horos"* (as already mentioned), *hypokeimenon*, and *katêgoroumenon* are the regular Aristotelian terms. Galen points this out when he says "following the old (*palaia*) usage." If the word *palaia* comes from Galen's source, it may indicate that the Stoic logicians used it in referring to Peripatetic expressions.

"For the sake of clear and concise exposition (*didaskalia*)" is an expression occurring often in Galen's writings, but also in Albinus, one of Galen's teachers. It seems to have been a cliché of the lecture hall and no doubt Galen picked it up during his years of assiduous attendance at the lectures of the leading professors of philosophy of his time. It expresses the ideal in exposition that Galen was guided by in all his writing.   It is terminology from the rhetorical schools.   According to Diogenes Laertius (Bk. VII sec. 59), Diogenes of Babylon listed five virtues of discourse: pure Greek, clarity, conciseness, propriety, and distinction.

Onoma and *rêma* as grammatical terms are found in Plato's *Phaedrus*, *Cratylus*, and *Sophist*.   In Plato *onoma* certainly means "noun," but *rêma* is somewhat more general, meaning something more like "predicate." Grammatical terminology was less settled in Plato's time.   In Aristotle's *de Interpretatione*, *rêma* comes closer to the sense of "verb," which it finally seems to have acquired in the Stoic and Alexandrian work of systematizing grammar.

Section 4

Up to this point, as we have seen, Galen's examples of propositions have all been of propositions with singulars as subjects.   He now has to introduce the propositions of the sort that categorical syllogisms are composed of, universals and particulars.   It must be remembered that in his exposition of the syllogism in *Prior Analytics* Aristotle never uses singular propositions.   Just as he introduced categorical propositions without mentioning categories, so here Galen introduces quantity of propositions without naming genera and species.   By a sort of operational definition he leads the student to the idea of subjects that may be "divided" and takes for granted that genera and species are understood.   The result is that the exposition here looks as if it were based on the modern notion of logic as a classification of sentences.   Since, however, we will soon find him violently objecting to Chrysippus's steps in this direction, it is more probable that he is using the pedagogical device of not intro-ducing complications before the student is ready for them.   On the other hand, in so far as Galen is working over already existing material, it may well be that the source or sources on which he is drawing took for granted the theory of genera and species and their accompaniments and wished to avoid the metaphysical questions which would arise if they were mentioned.

Section 5

There is a corruption of the MS. in the example of the universal negative.   After "No man" several letters are obscure, then follows *grapto*, which does not make sense.   Kalbfleisch suggests that something like *athanatos* is to be desired.   I have translated "painting," remembering Aristotle's use of *zôon* as an example of an equivocal term (*Cat.* 1 a 3).

Grapto suggests that some word for painting occurred in the text and left *grapto* as its trace.

The distinction affirmative and negative is introduced by example without definition, just as "category" was. The examples, of course, are no longer propositions with singular subjects. The mention of an alternative form of the particular negative is in keeping with the fact that Galen had written a book on equivalent propositions. Elsewhere in this work he returns to this subject. His position is simply that they are alternative ways of saying the same thing. The modern concern with equivalents would strike him as excessively formalistic.

The terminology of these propositions is Aristotelian. The names he uses for the propositions are all found in the first chapter of *Prior Analytics*. Galen's treatment omits Aristotle's indefinite premisses. These are defined in *de Interpretatione* as well as in *Prior Analytics*, but no use is made of them in setting up the syllogistic forms, since they are obviously nothing but incomplete propositions, having no sign of quantity. As the present work shows, they drop out of the tradition and little more is heard of them. Galen exemplifies the kinds of propositions with Aristotle's "man-animal" matrix of predication. He gives them in the ordinary form of sentences with *esti*, as Aristotle does in the corresponding discussion (*de Interp.*). Galen does not follow Aristotle's practice (*Anal. Pr.*) of putting propositions in the B *huparchei tôi* A form, which Aristotle uses almost exclusively in exhibiting the moods of the syllogism.

Section 6

This last sentence of Chapter II distinguishes singular propositions from quantified. The result of the distinction, whether realized or not, is to exclude singular propositions from use in the categorical syllogisms. This is Aristotle's practice in *Prior Analytics*, although he does admit in *Posterior Analytics* the example of predicating the genus animal of this man, if it is predicable of every man (*Anal. Post.*, 73 a 30). The present passage is not presenting a formal syllogism but is illustrating the meaning of "universal" and is discussing epistemology rather than logic.

In distinguishing species from individual, Galen's language departs from Aristotle's precision. "A substance defined not only according to species, but also according to number" seems to imply that individuals can be defined, which is contrary to Aristotle's position. The Aristotelian way of making the distinction is to speak of things that are one in species and of things that are one numerically. Galen's language seems to reflect a pedagogical succinctness, which loses some of the metaphysical precision, although conveying the idea sufficiently well for the purpose of an introduction. The participle "*horismenês*" probably should not be pressed too far in the direction of the meaning "definition." In any

case, the use of the term *ousia* here indicates that it has been smoothed
down to serve as a piece of scholastic jargon.

CHAPTER III

Section 1

Hypothetical propositions and the syllogisms formed from them were
systematized by the early Stoics, especially Chrysippus, after several
generations of polemic and discussion between the Peripatetic school and
the Megarians and Stoics.   The polemic lasted into the Greco-Roman
period, as is evidenced by remarks of Alexander.

Prantl, the nineteenth-century historian of logic, managed to confuse
the history of this development of thought.   By a strained interpretation
of certain passages in the later commentators on Aristotle, he reached the
unjustified conclusion that the traditional hypothetical syllogisms were
the discovery or invention of Theophrastus (Prantl, I, 386).   What seems
rather to be the case is that Theophrastus devoted study to questions
about arguments "from hypothesis" which were raised and declared
worthy of further study in a passage of the *Prior Analytics* (45 b 15–20).
In Aristotle's sense, hypothetical argument is a device for establishing
indirectly what cannot be directly proved owing to some deficiency in the
known data.   The term "hypothesis" points back to Plato's discussion
of the use of hypothesis in dialectic, as in the *Phaedo* (101 d) and *Meno*
(87 a).   The classification we find beginning here and developed in later
chapters is concerned with something different, the reasoning possible
from a given conditional or disjunctive relation of facts and the assertion
or denial of some one of these facts, reasoning dependent solely on the
nature of the conditional or disjunctive relation.   This is the branch of
logic called "propositional logic" by modern logicians.

It is for this reason that modern symbolic logicians find the Stoics to be
their forerunners.   In doing so, however, they overlook some important
aspects of the Stoic position.   What this position was will become clearer
in the discussion of later passages of the *Institutio*.   Galen himself takes
a controversial stance against the Stoics, and from his criticisms it is
possible to see in outline some of the points of agreement between them
and the symbolic logicians and some of the ways in which they differ.

In this section the conditional clauses of the translation render genitive
absolutes.   It would be better to render them by absolute constructions,
if the result were not nearly intolerable English, since the statements in
this section are an informal introduction of the notions which are defined
in the subsequent sections.

The terminology "hypothetical by connection" and "by separation" is
not found in Aristotle's logical works.   It is found in Alexander, generally
in connection with a criticism of the Stoic hypothetical syllogisms.

Alexander recognizes the equivalence of this terminology to the Stoic "conditional" and "disjunctive," but his criticism seems to miss the point that the Stoics are making.   Certain indications in Alexander's wording of his discussion seem to point to Theophrastus as the originator of the terminology that Galen calls Peripatetic.   On the other hand, certain other remarks of Alexander suggest that the establishment of the hypothetical syllogisms was accomplished by the Stoics and that he is using a terminology that originally had another reference in order to talk in Peripatetic terms about the Stoic syllogisms. (Alex. *in Anal. Pr.*, pp. 262–63.)

The terminology of propositions set forth in this section and the later sections of the chapter deserves closer study.   In the first place, although Galen is consistent in giving the Peripatetic name for conditional sentences as "hypothetical by connection," he gives the name for disjunctives first simply with the adjectival "separative," but later in section 4 as "hypothetical by separation."   He introduces the topic so as to suggest that he believed the Peripatetics had set up the term hypothetical as a name for the whole class of sentences consisting either of conditionals or disjunctives; this is certainly implied in the first sentence of this section and the contrasting prepositional phrases "by connection" and "by separation" name the two subclasses.   However, in his first statement of the distinction, the adjective "separative" seems to stand alone as a name for its class and not to be attached to "hypothetical."   Its form in *ikos* is parallel to "hypothetical."   It looks as if there was some variation in terminology in the Peripatetic school itself.   This is by no means surprising since even modern textbooks show the same indecision between using "hypothetical" as an inclusive term for conditionals and disjunctives, and sometimes conjunctive denial as well, and restricting it to sentences in the conditional form.

This problem about terms is unimportant in itself.   It has, however, a bearing on a more important question, the dispute between the Peripatetics and the Stoics about the foundations of logic.   Galen's notice of these terms is the earliest and most explicit we have.   Alexander uses them as part of the Peripatetic language in which he writes his commentary, and his usage supports Galen's statements.   The terms do not occur in Diogenes or Sextus.   Therefore, our text is of great importance if it can be made to yield information about the Peripatetic theories of hypothetical propositions and syllogisms.

I. M. Bochenski has argued (*La Log.*, p. 108) that since the Peripatetic terms are not Aristotelian, while the Stoic terms "conditional" and "disjunctive" are attested (in Diogenes Laertius) as being used, if not invented, by Chrysippus, the Peripatetic terms must stem from Theophrastus and Eudemus.   The two are usually mentioned together in the later references to logical matters.   Bochenski considers that Theophrastus is the only Peripatetic philosopher and logician between Aristotle and Chrysippus of sufficient stature to have established these terms so firmly in the tradition.   This argument is sound and is supported by references in Alexander and the other commentators, as well as Boethius, connecting Theophrastus and sometimes Eudemus, with the discussion of hypothetical reasoning.   It remains to be determined, if possible, what was the nature of Theophrastus's contribution, in addition to the invention of terms for the kinds of propositions.

This is not an easy question in the state of our sources of information. On the one hand we know that Aristotle refers (*Anal. Pr.*, 50 b 1) to arguments *ex hypotheseôs* and says that they stand in need of further investigation.   He sometimes links them to *reductio* arguments and occasionally gives an example of one.   The characteristic that emerges from the examples is of an argument in which, a direct proof being impossible, some hypothesis is assumed, from which the conclusion follows, and is consequently true, if the hypothesis is true.   It is evident that these arguments are not presented as logical forms, as are the categorical syllogisms, but as more or less *ad hoc* devices for dealing with special problems.   It is likely that Theophrastus, in following out his master's suggestions, and perhaps in connection with the classification of sentences as simple and complex (as in the *de Interpretatione*), adopted the term "hypothetical" for conditional sentences, from his observation that both Plato and Aristotle, when setting forth a hypothesis, frequently made use of the conditional form of sentence.   He probably further observed that the disjunctive sentence was also used in investigations starting from a dichotomy or *diaeresis*.   Perhaps he called this second form of sentence "separative" (*diaeretikê*) simply because it was used equally with hypothetical sentences as the starting point of an investigation.   Based on this argument, the terminology which spoke of hypothetical propositions subdivided into two kinds, connective and separative, would have evolved later.   It would have come about as scholars realized that there was a formal element to arguments *ex hypotheseôs*, which might be isolated just as the formal element of the categorical syllogism had been.   That this was the course things took is suggested by the terms themselves.   The term separative would have come easily from the Platonic term *diaeresis*, which signified the method of dichotomy with its natural form of expression in the disjunctive, e.g., "Animals are either rational or irrational."   The term "connection," however, is not the Platonic opposite of *diaeresis*; this is *synagogê*, (Plato, *Phaedrus*, 266 b 4), while the word connection is *synecheia* in Greek.   The latter is opposed to *diaeresis* in a physical sense, when there is the question of parts physically united or separated (cf. Aristotle, *de Partibus Animalium*, 654 b 16). It is possible then that the term "separative" established itself first, and when another term to name its co-ordinate subclass was wanted, *synecheia* suggested itself. Moreover, since Plato (*Sophist*, 262 c) had used the latter in discussing whether a sequence of words make a sentence or not, its use for a certain kind of proposition perhaps implies that the propositions were now being studied in their physical form as groups of words. In the final form of the theory, we may suppose, the term hypothetical retains its reference to the use of the proposition in a particular kind of reasoning, while the two distinguishing terms refer to the verbal form of expression. If this is so, we can see that Theophrastus is moving from the Aristotelian position to one that approaches the Stoic. The latter abandoned the term hypothetical altogether and substituted conjunctive and disjunctive as names for the two types.

Note: the Stoic *synemmenon* would be best translated "conjunctive" rather than "conditional" were it not that modern usage has pre-empted the term "conjunction" for a different kind of proposition, the Stoic *symploke*, that is the grammatical "compound sentence."

One further question that arises is whether the reduction of the two types of propositions to the position of subclasses of one "hypothetical" type may be due to the fact that Theophrastus had observed what Galen points out at the end of the present chapter, namely, that a conditional sentence is logically equivalent to a disjunctive in which the contradictory of the antecedent of the conditional is one of the members of the disjunction. If so, then Theophrastus had good formal grounds for establishing the general class of hypotheticals as including both conditionals and disjunctives.

Modern logicians distinguish two branches of logic: the propositional logic and the logic of terms. The latter is the logic of the Aristotelian categorical syllogism; in this the formal relations that make the cogency of the argument are relations between terms, the subjects and predicates of the premisses and conclusion of the categorical syllogism. On the other hand, the logic of propositions studies the formal pattern between whole propositions that portray various logical relationships, various conclusions that one is forced to draw from the relation between propositions indicated by the logical particles, "if," "and," "or," and "not." These particles are the distinguishing features in Galen's presentation of the Stoic logic. Galen himself tries, as the end of this chapter shows, to carry the distinction back from the verbal form to the material content of the proposition. It is a question whether Theophrastus ever freed himself from the Aristotelian point of view that logical relations were relations of terms and understood that the propositional logic is conducted on a different level. The view of Aristotle that hypothetical arguments were a device to deal with situations where knowledge of some terms was lacking probably prevented him from seeing that he was breaking ground in a new field of logic.

The evidence, exhaustively studied by Bochenski, suggests that

Theophrastus's work on "hypotheticals" was mainly devoted to the classification of this kind of proposition, rather than to the forms of argument into which they entered. The evidence, however, is far from complete. It is attested by Alexander (*in Anal. Pr.*, 326) and others that Theophrastus did formulate an argument called the "totally hypothetical" argument; but this is not a form within the propositional logic at all, but in effect, a categorical syllogism in which the predication of terms is admitted to be uncertain. It seems to be a precise formulation of one of the kinds of Aristotle's argument *ex hypotheseôs*. This would indicate that Theophrastus considered himself to be working within the old framework and that his classification of hypothetical propositions was designed to provide clear forms for use in more complex kinds of categorical syllogisms. There is no justification for Prantl's attempt to assign the discovery of the five indemonstrable hypothetical syllogisms, which do belong to the propositional logic, to Theophrastus.

Galen's statement, in informal manner, of the connective hypothetical includes the words "of necessity." This phrase implies that the term "if" expresses a necessary relation between the protasis and apodosis of a conditional sentence. In the generations after Theophrastus the question of the kind of necessary connection meant was argued at great length by logicians. We shall see traces of this discussion in the later portions of the *Institutio*. Galen seems clearly to find the necessity in the facts expressed in the clauses of the sentence, rather than in the verbal form, but the Stoics, although their doctrine is not entirely clear, seem to have focused on the verbal form and thereby won Galen's scorn. The same problem gave rise to another system of classification, which is not strictly logical, depending on the use of the conjunctions, *if, since,* and *because.* The difference between *ei, epei,* and *dioti,* for instance, is given by Diogenes Laertius (VII, 71f) as, according to Stoic doctrine, difference between a statement of hypothetical relation between antecedent and consequent, a statement of an inferential relation, and a statement of a causal relation. The first is true if the contradictory of its conclusion is incompatible with its antecedent; the second, if its antecedent is true and the conclusion follows from it; the third, if the conclusion follows from the antecedent, but not vice versa. Only the first of these forms is strictly a logical proposition. The second is an abbreviated form of the reasoning called *modus ponens*, while the third, as a statement of a causal relation, goes beyond logic entirely. Yet the parallelism of the propositions, both in ordinary language and in the philosophical treatment of them, is evidence of the tangle of notions that make up the idea of necessity, and illustrates the efforts that were made in the post-Aristotelian period to disentangle its separate meanings. On the evidence of Diogenes, it was the Stoics, and especially Chrysippus, who made this contribution to grammar and logic.

Section 2

This section contains a footnote explaining a meaning of a term used in the preceding text, followed by another note on a term in the first footnote. This kind of aside, filled with semantic matter, is characteristic of Galen. A similar note, dealing with the same terms, is found in *de Methodo Medico* (Kuehn, X, 155). There he asserts, against the *mikrologia* of some of the philosophers, "which they puffed themselves up about (*ekompseusanto*)," that there is no distinction in meaning between *to on* and *to hyphestêkos*. Those who practice this pettifoggery (certainly the Stoics) turn upside down the whole of everyday usage. His assertion here that the Greeks mean the same thing by the three terms is a similar appeal to customary usage.

Before *ê hyparchein, einai* is supplied by Kalbfleisch. Its presence is necessary to the thought. *Hyparchei* in the sense of the copula is prevalent in the *Prior Analytics*. Aristotle seems to have preferred the somewhat artificial form it gave to his syllogistic patterns, as concentrating attention on the form. *Hyphistemi* in the sense of "to be" occurs a few times in Aristotle but becomes frequent in Hellenistic and later philosophical writers. Its noun, *hypostasis*, was thus well suited to express Plotinus's theory of levels of being on which the emanations of the One settled themselves in their hierarchical descent to non-being. Although Galen seems to overaccent the semantic relations of the terms in this note, they are important in logical structure. He thus gives himself license to vary his expressions in the rest of the discussion. The occasion for the note is his use of *hyparxeôs* in the preceding section. It is somewhat odd that he appends this note to a sentence describing the kind of propositions that are not concerned with *hyparxis*. Odder still, at first sight, is the fact that in Chapter XIV, 1, Galen asserts that arguments based on hypothetical propositions are used in investigations of the *hyparxis* of things. There is, however, no paradox. Here *hyparxis* is used, in obvious recollection of *Prior Analytics*, for the reference of categorical *propositions*, that is, those in which a predicate is asserted of a subject. The hypotheticals are to be distinguished as asserting a relation between propositions, not the inherence of a predicate in a subject. In Chapter XIV, as in the first section of Chapter II, *hyparxis* is used as a term for "existence" simply as prior to determinate predication of the categorical kind.

In the second semantic note of the section terms of importance in logic, or at least the epistemological background of logic, are discussed, with a very forced relevance to the immediate context. The distinction drawn between *ennoia* and *noêsis* is far from clear, and, in fact, Galen does not himself always observe the distinction. For instance, in the sentences immediately following those quoted from *de Methodo Medendi* he uses the terms synonymously. It is puzzling that in the first part of this section he insists on the words he is dealing with being synonyms, while in this case he makes a rather strained distinction. It looks as if he has been rather carried away by his lifelong enthusiasm for semantic analysis.

Some light is thrown on Galen's meaning by a passage from Plutarch, cited by Kalbfleisch (*Which Animals are Intelligent*? 961 c): *hosper . . . ta peri tas noêseis, has enapokeimenas men "ennoias" kalousi, kinoumenas de "dianoêseis."* Plutarch, however, seems to be distinguishing concepts simply held in mind from concepts actually in use in thinking, while Galen seems to be talking of concepts of different kinds of objects. Since Galen is making a cursory observation, he may not have expressed himself with sufficient care, or he may not have understood the distinction, which no doubt was a commonplace in the teaching of logic. He seems, moreover, to have been interested in the connection of the term *ennoia* with the Aristotelian "axiom," as in Euclid's *koinai ennoiai*, a term which also had a role in Stoicism. This is noted in Galen's word *emphutoi*.

The placing of these footnotes interrupts the exposition of hypothetical propositions. It suggests the possibility in respect to the composition of the *Institutio* that Galen was working from a handbook of logic into which he interspersed his own comments on occasion. The tone and content of this section is plainly Galenic and could hardly have stood in the kind of formal exposition of elementary logic that the rest of the chapter points to.

Section 3

This section owes its confusing appearance to the fact that Galen is attempting to be "clear and concise" about three separate matters:

1. Hypothetical propositions themselves, that is, as we have seen, propositions that combine two or more categorical propositions by means of logical conjunctions.

2. The difference between the terminology of the Peripatetics and of the Stoics.

3. The fact that the two kinds of hypothetical propositions he is considering may be expressed by the two logical particles "if" and "or," and also, with the help of negation, may each be expressed with either one of these particles.

3a. A subordinate fact is noticed: that the logical particles each have, in Greek, two forms, an emphatic and an unemphatic.

Strictly speaking, hypothetical propositions have already been defined and named with the Peripatetic terms in the first section. The resumptive *men oun* shows that he is returning to the subject after the footnotes of section 2. He can thus express the already presented form shortly with a genitive introduced by *dia*. *Dia* in effect repeats the *ex anankês* of section 1; it is not to be understood as including causal clauses as possible elements in hypothetical propositions.

The difference between Peripatetic and Stoic terminology reflects their different understanding of the propositions, as we have already explained. For the Peripatetics, apparently, the distinction is made between "connective" and "separative" hypotheticals by the fact that in the former the antecedent clause is affirmative, in the latter, negative. The Peripatetics thus carried the distinction back to the meaning of the proposition. The Stoics, on the other hand, distinguished the same two kinds by expressing the first with "if" and the second with "or." They established in this way a verbal distinction corresponding to the material distinction of the content of the proposition. This enabled them to handle the propositions as formal elements in arguments with greater clarity. Galen objects, at the end of the present chapter, to this formalism of the Stoics. For him, the function of logic is to construct demonstrations which the scientist uses; one's attention is to be given to the facts about which one is reasoning, not to the form in which those facts are stated. Galen, however, remains true to his purpose in writing this book, which is to give the terminology of both the schools.

There is considerable difficulty with the last clause of this section; in the first place the text is unsound, and secondly, the task of translation encounters obstacles perhaps due to a carelessness of phrasing. Since I have departed from Kalbfleisch's text in my translation, I shall first give it, together with the MS. readings from which he deviates and then attempt to justify my translation.

> *oikeiotera de esti lexis to [ta] diezeugmenon tois axiômasi has dêlonoti diairetikas protaseis ephamen onomazesthai, dia tou êtoi sundesmou— diapherei de ouden "ê" dia mias sullabês ê dia duoin— ê tois sunêmmenois dia tou ei [ê epei], eiper hen kai houtoi sêmainousi.*
> line 1: Ms. *diezeugmena*, line 2: *dêlonoti* ex *dêlon* corr. P conicias *dê*, line 4: *ê* coni. Kalb.; *ê epei*, coni. Prantl. also, for *ê* ad init. Prantl reads *eti*.

Kalbfleisch's text seems to require the translation: "'Disjunctive' is the more suitable expression for the propositions, which . . ., through 'or' . . . than to the conditionals through 'if'. . . ."

This translation is impossible for several reasons. In the first place, the word *lexis* is used frequently in the *Institutio* and always for a sentence or clause or phrase, never for a term. Therefore, he cannot be calling "disjunctive" a *lexis*. More important, it is nonsense to say that "disjunctive" is a more suitable expression for propositions constructed with "or," than for conditionals.   Since the "than" of Kalbfleisch's text is his conjecture, it need not be retained.

In order to discover the meaning of the sentence and to establish a text, the following may be proposed.   According to Kalbfleisch's apparatus the MS. shows immediately after *synêmmenois* a *dê* corrected in another hand to *ê* ("or").   With this to go on, a simple change to *hê* (fem. def. art.) would warrant an insertion of another *hê* before *dia tou êtoi*.   This phrase may then be taken as the subject of *esti*, making *oikeioīera lexis* the predicate.   The textual confusion *to ta diezeugmena* strongly suggests that these words result from a gloss, and that the term "disjunctive" did not occur at all in Galen's sentence.   Some reader glossed *tois axiomasi* with it.   The comparison then looks back to the preceding clause, in which the "separative" or "disjunctive" proposition is given in the form of a hypothetical with negative antecedent.   Galen would then be indicating a preference for the use of "or" to express disjunctives, and as an afterthought, the use of "if" to express conditionals.   Prantl's conjecture of *eti* before *synêmmenois* would keep the construction straight, although *kai* or *hosper kai* would do better, if their loss could be accounted for.   Possibly a simple *hôs* might be easily lost.

In the last line of text the words *ê epei* are a conjecture of Prantl.   The justification for them is that *epei* is attested by Diogenes Laertius and others as the conjunction introducing a so-called *parasunêmmenon*, which differs from the conditional introduced by *ei* in that it implies that the protasis of the sentence is true.   Thus it is conceivable that Galen was thinking of the two conjunctions as essentially signifying the same logical relation.   On the other hand, *ei* and *eiper* do not differ in logical function, and in this respect are similar to the two forms of the disjunctive particle. It is hard to suppose that Galen could have meant that *ei* and *epei* mean the same.   Furthermore, the immediately following *eiper* would easily account for the loss of the first one.

Further support for the conjecture *eiper* may be found in Sextus Empiricus (*Adv. Math.*, VIII, 109).   Sextus announces a treatment of non-simple sentences.   He takes up first the conditional and says:

> *lambanesthô de ek toutôn epi tou parontos to kaloumenon synêmmenon. touto toinun synestêken ex axiômatos diaphoroumenou ê ex axiômatôn dia tou 'ei' ê 'eiper' syndesmou.* . . .

Section 5

This last section points out the already implied equivalence between a conditional with negative antecedent and a disjunctive.   The repetition with the subjects of protasis and apodosis interchanged is owing to the fact that the order of members in a disjunctive is immaterial, while in a conditional protasis must precede apodosis (logically, not grammatically).

Galen reveals something of his conception of logic by making the question of what to call the proposition depend on the relation of fact signified by the proposition rather than upon the grammatical form. In so doing, he ranges himself with Theophrastus, we may suppose, and against the Stoics. It seems most probable that the latter are those who attend to the words alone, since both in the *Institutio* and elsewhere he makes similar charges against the Stoics. It is noteworthy that he nevertheless uses the Stoic terminology to refer to the logical form, in spite of the Peripatetic point of view that he favors (cf. Alex. *in Anal. Pr.*, p. 372.29).

One point to be noted is that for the Stoics, and for Galen in this work, the disjunctive proposition expresses the exclusive sense of "or." The member propositions of the disjunctive can neither be true at the same time, nor false at the same time. Therefore, both conditionals have to be stated to bring out this fact.

The last statement is not completely accurate. If two propositions are combined in an exclusive disjunction, then the relation between one of them and the contradictory of the other must be a relation of exact equivalence, not of simple implication. That Galen was aware of this is clear from his later discussion of the fourth and fifth indemonstrable syllogisms of Chrysippus. In effect, these two syllogisms show that, given an exclusive disjunction, if one member is true, the second is false and if the first member is false, the second is true. Combining these two conclusions, it follows that the truth of one implies the falsehood of the other and vice versa, that is, one member is true, if, and only if, the other is false. There seems to be no logical particle to express this equivalence, or mutual implication, except by using a pair of conditionals with inverse placing of the member propositions in protasis and apodosis. Galen's discussion presents the inverse pairs of conditionals but, by keeping the negative in the apodosis in each case, he has not shown mutual implication, but only the equivalence generated by the operation called contraposition. This consists of denying the consequent of a conditional, making it the antecedent of another conditional with the negation of the first antecedent as consequent. The same implication is stated in the new form as in the old. In mutual implication, on the other hand, each separate implication is different, and the resulting statement signifies another fact of implication.

Father James W. Stakelum (*Galen and the Logic of Propositions*, pp. 46–54) has brought out, first, that this section does imply the relation of exclusive disjunction to mutual implication of one member and the contradictory of the other, and secondly, that in the following discussion of conflict and consequence, Galen has shown this relation. He seems, however, not to have considered sufficiently that the presentation in this section is defective. Therefore, he gives Galen somewhat more credit for making an interesting logical discovery than may be warranted.

Discussion of conflict and consequence must wait for the next chapter. Here is further comment on what Galen's words in this section reveal about the knowledge of logical forms and operations that he held or that is implied in the background against which he was working. He indicates that it was possible to look on the logical tradition available to him as divided between two points of view. On the one hand, there is the verbal or formalist view, which he rejects, which named the elements of the science according to the linguistic expression of meanings; and on the other, the view which looks to the nature of the facts in order to discover the relations upon which inferences could be founded. From information Galen gives us in this work, as well as from sources such as Sextus, Diogenes, and Alexander, it is reasonable to label these points of view Stoic and Peripatetic, respectively. It is well to keep in mind, however, that these labels simply mean that they were so considered by Galen and those from whom Galen learned logic. We cannot be sure that the point of view of Chrysippus was exactly what the early Christian centuries took to be the Stoic point of view, nor that the point of view of Theophrastus and Eudemus was identical with the traditional Peripatetic position. It seems probable that by Galen's time discussion of logic had fully clarified and distinguished the points of view. In the earlier time, no doubt, they were not so distinct. Certainly Aristotle's *Topics* deals at times with logical connections and exclusions but always presented through examples and with a terminology that leaves the above mentioned distinction unclear. Theophrastus, it is reasonable to suppose, in systematizing his master's doctrines, invented more technical terms to handle the discussion. In this way he would have prepared the road for Chrysippus to arrive at his formalistic logic. Once complex propositions were classified and named, it was easier to see that the logical relations they could imply belonged more to the form than to the content of the propositions. No doubt the different metaphysical positions of the Stoics and the Peripatetics inclined the former to their propositional logic, while the Peripatetic notions of a world of genera and species, with their properties and accidents, kept the latter bent toward emphasizing the logical relations of terms. This whole point will be discussed more fully in connection with a later chapter of the *Institutio*.

CHAPTER IV

Sections 1 and 2

The doctrine of consequence and conflict presented in this chapter shows signs of being a long-established and carefully constructed theory. Its source is somewhat obscure. Prantl (I, 596) simply asserts, without giving much support to his statement, that the term "*machē*" is a Stoic term. Schmekel (I, 536) asserts that Chrysippus had probably made the doctrine of consequence and conflict the foundation of his proposition and syllogism theory, but only in attention to the external form, or material relation and verbal expression, not taking into consideration the logical relations of the members of propositions.

Evidence from which to answer the question about these terms is scanty. In fact, it is perhaps not altogether clear what precisely the question is. There are several questions. The simplest is: When and by whose agency did *akolouthia* and *machê* become technical, logical terms? Second, what is their logical significance? And third, what is their connection with the indemonstrable hypothetical syllogisms?

In Plato the Greek terms occur occasionally, used in their ordinary sense, but within a logical context. *Akolouthia* or the verb is used of statements that are consistent with one another (e.g., *Gorgias*, p. 457), but apparently never in the developed sense of logical implication. *Machomai* occurs at *Theaetetus*, 155b, in an assertion that three admitted statements (*homologemata*) conflict "in our souls." The words, however, are, as usual in Plato, used untechnically. They are not connected with the conditional or disjunctive form of expression, although they might have been.

Aristotle seems to have advanced *akolouthia* to a more technical status, but not to have used *machê* in this way. In *Topics* (114b), *akolouthia* is used of the relation of a property to its possessor, with the intention of showing that this relation may be used to establish an implication which may support one's own argument or refute that of an opponent. But the meaning of the term is attached to the relations of the things under discussion rather than of statements about the things.

Nevertheless, as a result of Aristotle's usage, this term at least was ready to go over to the purely logical field and no doubt it was from him that the Stoics derived the term, directly, or through Theophrastus. Their investigation of complex sentences in their logical aspects, the continuance of Theophrastus's study of hypothetical propositions and arguments, must have been the occasion for the fixing of the terms into a technical sense. They were aided in their classification by the square of oppositions. The terms became metalinguistic devices for talking about the logical relations of conditionals and disjunctives.

There is a difficulty in this account. Galen uses the doctrine of *akolouthia* and *machê* as a means of criticizing Chrysippus's formulation of the hypotheticals. For him, they describe the state of affairs (*physis tôn pragmatôn*) rather than the relations of clauses in a complex sentence and give meaning to the form of the sentence. On the other hand, the kinds of consequence and conflict are closely related to the five indemonstrable syllogisms of Chrysippus. It looks as if Chrysippus had invented the five indemonstrables and had used consequence and conflict as terms to talk about these forms, while Galen or his predecessors had referred them back, in the manner of Aristotle, to the things signified in the hypothetical propositions, thus giving to the latter a basis in what seemed to them to be a natural and non-linguistic set of relations. The doctrine presented by Galen is certainly more sophisticated and more precise than anything we can discover in Aristotle's use of the terms, but it is permeated with a Peripatetic point of view.

This doctrine is certainly not invented by Galen. We meet a version of it in Cicero's *Topics*. There he speaks of *consequentia, antecedentia,* and *repugnantia,* terms which are met with elsewhere in the tradition of Roman rhetoric. He connects them with a set of seven indemonstrables which are Chrysippus's with one duplication, and one that is logically fallacious in any system of logic. It is clear that Cicero's understanding of logic is defective. Nevertheless, his passage has value because it establishes the fact that the doctrine of consequence and conflict was a part of formal Stoic instruction in logic. This follows from a comparison of a remark at the end of the *Topics* (pp. 14, 57) "in quo est tota fere dialectice," with *Brutus*, p. 309, after mention of Diodotus the Stoic, continuing "A quo cum in aliis rebus tum studiossime in dialectica exercebar, quae quasi contracta et astricta eloquentia putanda est." Cicero, then, learned "dialectic" from Diodotus, and we hear of no other teacher, and the doctrine summarized (*Top.*, pp. 12, 53ff) is almost the whole of the dialectic. Therefore, the Chrysippean indemonstrables as well as the doctrine of consequence and conflict were the Stoic tradition in the teaching of logic.

There are, indeed, striking differences between Cicero's handling of this doctrine and that which we find in the *Institutio*. First, while Galen and other sources speak of consequence and conflict, Cicero speaks of consequence, antecedence, and conflict (*consecutio, antecessio* and *repugnantia*). In the sequel he plainly equates consequence with Chrysippus's first indemonstrable syllogism, antecedence with his second, and conflict with a certain form of his third, namely conjoint denial of two propositions, one affirmative and one negative. After an irrelevant disquisition on a rhetorical elaboration of the last-named, he goes on to list Chrysippus's fourth and fifth syllogisms as based on disjunctions and adds a sixth and seventh which are the same as Chrysippus's third, without the negative member, and a fallacious analogue of the third in which the minor is the denial of one of the members.

The introduction of antecedence reveals a different understanding of the meaning of the terms. Apparently he takes consequence as a name for the hypothetical syllogism (Chrysippus's first) which proves the consequent by affirming the antecedent. Conversely the second disproves the antecedent by denying the consequent (hence the name "antecedence"). In the case of the third, he seems to justify the term "conflict" by the fact that an affirmative and negative are conjoined.

This whole understanding is at variance with Galen's use of the terms, for Galen means consequence and conflict to refer not to hypothetical syllogisms but to hypothetical propositions, and his explanation is that the terms refer to the state of affairs signified in the propositions, from which state of affairs the necessity of the conclusions of the five indemonstrables follows. In Galen, all five syllogisms are shown to derive their cogency from the significance of their major, hypothetical premisses.

A minor difference in Cicero's treatment is that he gives as an example for the first three syllogisms a situation drawn from Roman law, instead of the Stoic play with day and night. The last four forms are given not through an example but with pronouns illustrating schematically the separate forms.

At first one is tempted to suppose that Diodotus taught Cicero an interesting variation of Chrysippus's doctrine and to speculate on when this variation separated from the doctrine as it was handed down to Galen. When one remembers, however, Cicero's words in the introduction to the *Topics* (I, 5), "memoria repetita in ipsa navigatione conscripsi," one suspects that some of the variation is due to faulty memory. Indeed, it may be possible that the fallacious form of conjoint denial was remembered from one of the times when Cicero "threw dust in the eyes of the judges" rather than from the lectures of Diodotus.

Cicero's statements do, however, show that a doctrine of consequence and conflict was part of the Stoic curriculum in Dialectic and that in it they were connected with the indemonstrable syllogisms. This is exactly what we find in Galen. A closer link with Galen is found in Albinus's *Introduction to Plato's Philosophy*. Albinus was one of Galen's teachers. His extant summaries of Platonic philosophy are heavily contaminated with Stoic terminology and Stoic teaching. In chapter VI (*Platonis Dialogi*, VI, 158) Albinus summarizes Plato's use of logic and gives a brief account of technical logic, discussing first categorical propositions and then hypothetical. Of the latter he says, "Those that reveal consequence or conflict are hypothetical propositions." He does not define consequence and conflict but goes on to list the figures of the categorical syllogisms, the totally hypothetical and the "mixed," which are the Chrysippean indemonstrables. In discussing these latter he gives an example of a "constructive syllogism derived from consequence" drawn from Plato's *Parmenides*, and sketches its completion in the Stoic manner of giving a rule of inference. He follows this with a "destructive syllogism from consequence" but does not complete its explanation and he says nothing about syllogisms from conflict. (The terms "constructive" and "destructive" derive from Aristotle's *Topics*.) He has said enough, however, to show that the relation of the doctrine of consequence and conflict to the indemonstrables is so well established that it can be referred to without explicit development. It is thus probable that Galen learned from Albinus the doctrine he begins to expound in this chapter. This supposition is supported by the fact that the examples used to illustrate categorical syllogisms recur practically word for word later in the appropriate part of the *Institutio*. Albinus's treatment, however, shows all the signs of relying on an earlier handbook for its arrangement and examples, so that the conclusion to be drawn is at most that Galen drew on the textbook recommended by his teacher when he came to write the present treatise. There is, moreover, a major difference between Galen's treatment and Albinus's. The latter includes between the Aristotelian syllogisms and the Chrysippean the "totally hypothetical syllogisms" of Theophrastus. These nowhere are mentioned in Galen. Either they were not included in the supposed textbook or Galen or an earlier editor of the textbook had seen that they were strictly speaking not a special kind of syllogism and removed them. If this removal is due to Galen himself, it speaks for his logical competence.

A study of the fragmentary evidence as to the use of the terms "consequence" and "conflict" throws doubt on Prantl's assertions that they are Stoic terms. Indeed, the evidence points rather the other way, that they are terms used outside the Stoic school, by writers who discuss the dialectic of Chrysippus and try, as Galen does, to relate it to the syllogistic of Aristotle. Thus in Diogenes Laertius's account in Book VII of Stoic logic the nouns do not occur and the verbs are used in their general sense. Sextus Empiricus's usage is very similar. These two authors depend, in the passages in question, on direct Stoic sources. On the other hand, this passage of Galen certainly uses the nouns as technical terms naming something represented by the Stoic hypothetical propositions; likewise, as has just been pointed out, Albinus, Galen's Platonist teacher, states exactly the same doctrine, while Alexander of Aphrodisias in many passages indicates that he is following the same teaching. The evidence of Cicero's *Topics*, for what it is worth, also comes from a writer who combined learning in Stoicism with a leaning to a Peripatetic Platonism.

There is one piece of evidence from Alexander's commentary on the *Prior Analytics* which supports this view. He says (p. 373, 28, Wallies) that though the Stoics admit that the expression "If A, then B and A, therefore B" is equivalent to "B is consequent upon A," the former is syllogistic, but the latter is not, but "perantic." This distinction points up the formalism of the Stoics, but it also seems to indicate that the Stoic who made the comment was replying to someone holding Galen's view, that the conditional expressed a state of affairs called "consequence" and that this was the logical significance of the conditional. For the Stoics, the use of the term "consequence" was a loose, metalinguistic way of talking about what they conceived to be exactly expressed in the conditional.

The closest association between the Stoic formalism and one of the terms in question, "conflict," occurs in a sentence found in Bekker's *Anecdota Graeca* (p. 484). It calls attention to "A difference made by the Stoics in sentences disjunctive by nature between 'being in conflict' and being in 'contradiction'"; that which cannot be used of the same subject is "in conflict"... e.g. "It is day or it is night," or, "I speak or I am silent," *et similia*. But the negated sentence is "in contradiction."

The conclusion that may be drawn from the evidence cited is that the Stoics did use the verbs *akoloutheô* and *machomai* to talk about the relations between the clauses of conditional and disjunctive sentences, but that they used them more or less informally and did not work out the kind of theory of conflict and consequence which Galen presents. The use of the nouns related etymologically to the verbs is confined to non-Stoic sources or is at least more frequent there, and this use of the nouns is a sign of the articulation of a system or theory. Galen's report of the theory, which is the only one we have, bears obvious resemblance to the pattern of relationships found in the Aristotelian "square of oppositions" and no doubt represents a Peripatetic attempt to bring the theory of Chrysippus about hypothetical propositions into the scheme of Aristotelian logic. Galen's insistence that the Stoics do not pay attention to the "state of affairs" but only to the linguistic form (whether he correctly interprets the Stoics or not) indicates that he is following the Peripatetic position.

Some further support for this statement may be found in the last section of the preceding chapter. There Galen asserted the equivalence of the disjunctive form with "or" to the conditional with a negated antecedent. Perhaps significantly he refers to the disjunctive, in saying that it is equivalent to the conditional with negative antecedent, by the term "separative premiss" which he has just told us is the Peripatetic term for this kind of proposition. Accordingly, it looks as if he is drawing this bit of doctrine from a Peripatetic source.

There is one further difficulty with the doctrine of these sections, which may be due to the supposed source or may be Galen's own doing. We have seen that he makes the disjunctive, expressing "complete conflict," equivalent to a conditional with negative antecedent. Strictly, this is only a partial equivalence, since, on Galen's definition of complete conflict, a conditional with negative consequent would also be consonant with the facts asserted in the disjunctive; i.e., from "Either it is day or it is night," follows by immediate inference, "If it is day, it is not night." But Galen asserts in section 1 of this chapter that the conditional with negative consequent expresses incomplete conflict, what he later says is usually expressed by the "not both" form. This is, of course, true and is probably the reason that he does not connect this form with the disjunctive. His example is "If Dion is in Athens, he is not at the Isthmus," which of course does not fit into the disjunctive form (Dion might be in Rome). But then, the conditional with negative consequent is ambiguously situated with relations to the kinds of conflict. Part of the difficulty is inherent in the ambiguity of the conjunction "or." Galen, following Chrysippus, treats it as expressing what modern logicians call "exclusive alternation," i.e., "Either p or q, but not both," and which they reject from their primary forms in favor of non-exclusive alternation, i.e., "At least one of p or q and maybe both." Treating the disjunctive in this way restores the full equivalence to the conditional with negative antecedent. We have seen that Father Stakelum recognized that exclusive disjunction required the assumption that the conditional be a biconditional ("if and only if") and credited Galen with this anticipation of modern logic. One may equally well look at the other side of the coin and credit Galen with the discovery of non-inclusive alternation. This cannot really be done, however, since Galen's definition of complete conflict makes it perfectly clear that he means exclusive alternation by his disjunctive. At any rate, these difficulties no doubt reflect the awkwardness of trying to accommodate the Stoic logic to Peripatetic ideas. Galen would probably reply that the "state of affairs" (*phusis tôn pragmatôn*) distinguishes between complete and incomplete conflict; but this is to introduce extraneous criteria into the science of logic at a point where accuracy of form is still possible.

At the end of section 2, Mau deletes the negative, making the assertion that one must be true, which is, of course, the mark of complete conflict. However, the negative does not make the sentence meaningless, since conflict also means that one of the members of the disjunction is false or non-existent.

Galen introduces here, solely to exemplify the meaning of conflict, the fourth, fifth, and third indemonstrable syllogisms of Chrysippus. They are discussed fully in Chapters XIV and XV.

I have translated Galen's "syllogism" in the first line by "scheme of argument," since the technical sense of the word syllogism is only later defined.

The last clause of the sentence is an etymological note. *Prolêpsis*, "assumption," was the Stoic technical term for the minor or second premiss of a hypothetical syllogism, the assertion or denial of one of the members of the hypothetical major premiss. It is called *proslêpsis* because one "takes it in addition" (*proslambanei*) to the asserted major (cf. Alex. *in Anal. Pr.*, 19, 3; 263, 26ff).

Section 4

This paragraph is difficult to understand without what follows, both in this chapter and later, in Chapter XIV, where Galen explicitly states his objection to the third indemonstrable of Chrysippus. Galen's objection is that the third indemonstrable depends on joining two incompatibles and denying their conjunction. Chrysippus, because of his formalistic way of describing sentences, makes such a proposition indistinguishable from the denial of any compound sentence, though it be one in which the assertions made in the separate clauses are not in themselves incompatible.

The obscurity of Galen's argument is at least partly due to his not having available a sufficiently precise grammatical terminology. His first example shows a single subject with a compound predicate (Dion is not both in Athens and on the Isthmus); his second, two clauses with different subjects (Dion is walking and Theon is talking). If Galen means that the subject of both clauses must be the same in order for there to be incompatibility between them, he has made a mistake. For "Electricity is the cause of lightning and Zeus hurls thunderbolts" is a compound sentence with separate subjects in each clause and separate predicates, which, however, contains incomplete conflict, i.e., both clauses cannot be true and yet both may be false.

I take *eph heterón phónón* to mean "expressed in two complete and distinct clauses." Granting that *phoné* generally means "word," in this text, it could mean phrase or clause. *Phónón* is Kalbfleisch's emendation of *phonén*; *heterón* then would mean subjects. The essential meaning is the same.

Whether Galen's criticism of the third indemonstrable is well taken or not must be left for later consideration. Certainly the denial of Dion walking and Theon talking, together with the assertion of either clause, entails the denial of the other clause. However, the assertion of Dion walking and Theon talking can be true, while the assertion that Dion is both in Athens and on the Isthmus is, in the nature of the case, self-contradictory. In the case of complete conflict, "Either p or q, but not both," the assertion, "Both p and q," and the assertion, "Neither p nor q," are necessarily false, if the assertion "Either p or q, but not both," is true. This is clear from the form of the expression, without regard to the content. It seems invalid for Galen to make the case of incomplete conflict depend on a reference to the state of affairs, when no such reference is necessary in the other case. That is to say, the expression "not both . . ." seems to have its own logical force, whatever the values that are substituted for the clauses in the conjunction. Galen, nevertheless, may have considered that the validity of a form depends upon the inconsistency of its contradictory and thus only the form "Dion is not both at Athens and on the Isthmus" would satisfy his criterion of validity.

Galen's position with regard to incomplete conflict again shows a certain Peripatetic leaning. What it amounts to is that a subject cannot have two inconsistent accidental predicates at the same time. If this is the correct interpretation, then he does not see that Chrysippus is dealing with propositional logic rather than predicational logic.

Sections 5, 6, 7

These sections discuss grammatical terminology, specifically the name for the kind of proposition he has been dealing with.   Two forms seem to have been in current use and as usual Galen declares that minor points of expression are irrelevant as long as clarity is maintained.   This gives him an opportunity to blast the pettifoggery of Chrysippus and at the same time to accuse him of blurring distinctions that are important. Finally he appends a brief note on "consequent," giving several synonyms and asserting that they all are metaphors from daily life.   Somewhat irrelevantly he adds that there are several kinds of "consequence" as well as of "conflict," which it is the business of the theory of proof to investigate.   Another sign of possible Peripatetic influence is his use of *nomothetountes* in the sense of assigning meaning to a word.   This recalls a sentence in *Posterior Analytics* (83 a 14), but it is closer to Sextus (*Adv. Math.*, VIII, 125).

CHAPTER V

Section 1

In this section Galen deals with the possibility of disjunctive propositions having more than two members.   Sextus and Diogenes, in reporting the doctrine of Chrysippus, illustrate disjunctives with two-membered propositions only.   The extension to more than two does not affect the doctrine.   It does, however, offer the pretty case of a multi-membered disjunctive's being reduced to a quasi-disjunctive.

More important is Galen's recognition of several kinds of disjunction or alternation.   In addition to the Stoic disjunctive, which is the excluding alternation of modern logic, where only one of the alternatives can be true, Galen recognizes the near-disjunctive, the incomplete conflict of the last chapter, where all the alternatives may be false, but not more than one can be true.

The paradisjunctive presents a problem for Galen's classification. Although it is expressed in disjunctive form and embodies the word "disjunctive" in its name, it does not, according to Galen, express conflict but incomplete consequence. (We learn this in Chapter XV, where there is an incorrect reference to this chapter implying that this fact had been stated here.) The state of affairs expressed is what modern logicians call non-excluding alternation: one of the alternatives must be true and more than one or all may be true. This is incomplete consequence in Galen's sense, because that is defined as the situation of statements that may be true together but cannot all be false together.

This passage brings to light an awkwardness in Galen's attempt to base the Stoic formulas for the indemonstrable syllogisms in consequence and conflict. While the particles "or" and "not both" serve well to distinguish complete and incomplete conflict (taking "or" in the sense of "aut" rather than "vel"), the particle "if" does not, in its usual acceptation, express either complete consequence or incomplete. We have seen already that Stakelum shows that complete consequence must be expressed by "if and only if," that is the modern biconditional, while incomplete consequence is expressed by the modern non-exclusive alternation ("vel"). This latter is not true for Stakelum, for whom incomplete consequence is the material conditional. The conditional expresses something more complex; if the first member is true, the second must be, and if the second is false, the first must be also. Galen, of course, has said this, but he leaves unstated the difficulty this fact raises for the symmetry of his doctrine. The difficulty may be expressed in other words by saying that in the disjunctive the order of the members is indifferent, while in the simple conditional the order is essential to the meaning of the sentence.

The mention of the paradisjunctive in this place raises another kind of problem. The next section, introduced by a *gar* proceeds to illustrate the structure of a quasi-disjunctive. The example Galen gives is the same as one given by Aulus Gellius (*Attic. Nights.*, ch. 8, sec. 14) to illustrate what Gellius calls a "paradisjunctive." Since Gellius is discussing Stoic terminology in this chapter and seems to be quoting a Stoic source, it is evident that Galen is giving a different and possibly non-Stoic sense to the word. His definition of paradisjunctive has therefore apparently intruded itself into a discussion that relies on a Stoic source. The fact that Galen devotes the whole of Chapter XV to the structure and use of the paradisjunctive shows that he was aware of the difficulty. Whether his false reference to this passage indicates that something has fallen out here, or is just Galen's memory playing him false is uncertain.

Stakelum (p. 38) argues that Galen is combining the Aristotelian treatment of contradictories and contraries, as given in the *Categories* and *De Interpretatione*, with the Stoic doctrine of disjunctives. It is true that since he does not follow the Stoics in fixing a completely formal meaning for the disjunctive particle he has to rely on a reference to the content of his propositions in order to distinguish to what class any one belongs. And we have seen that he creates a difficulty for himself in the case of incomplete conflict by refusing to call it a negative conjunction. Galen was familiar with the *Categories* and the other books of the *Organon*, so that it is not unlikely that he thought in Peripatetic terms. He does not, however, adopt the Aristotelian terminology of contradictories and contraries, but he seems to feel that he can adhere up to a point to the Stoic terminology, without going all the way with their formalism. A possible explanation of this fact is that, as examples later in the book seem to show, he is thinking of his own practice as an anatomical and medical investigator, and assumes that the user of logic, being a scientist in a special field, has a close enough command of his empirical findings that the Aristotelian doctrine in all its elaboration is not necessary for keeping the material straight, while Stoic formalism has the advantage of greater simplicity and clarity of expression.

Section 2

Simple propositions, here and at the end of the preceding section, mean a single predication of a single subject, what modern logicians call "atomic propositions."

Galen's example shows that he understands a disjunctive to be composed of mutually exclusive members that exhaustively enumerate the possible predicates, within a certain field of predication. If the members are not mutually exclusive, the result is a paradisjunctive; if they do not enumerate exhaustively, there is a quasi-disjunctive expressing incomplete conflict. It is from the nature of the facts signified that the form of disjunction is determined. The ambiguity of the disjunctive particle prevents the recognition of the kind from the form alone. It is uncertain whether the Stoics had progressed so far in formalism as to legislate a restricted meaning for the disjunctive particle; Galen seems to imply that they had.

Sections 3 and 4

This passage illustrates the difficulty of trying to express a logical situation without an accurate symbolism. What Galen seems to mean is that if one is given three or more simple propositions related in complete conflict, the affirmation of one of them necessarily entails the conjoint denial of the rest; that is, if the first is true, then neither the second nor the third or so on can be true. Similarly, denying that the second and the third, etc., are true means that the first is true. But, on the other hand, the denial of the first does not allow the assertion that the second *and* the third, etc., are true. One might suppose the possibility that the denial of the first leaves the second *or* the third. Similarly, we cannot say that the second and the third are true (since the original condition is that only one of the propositions is true) and therefore that the first is not true. Here, too, the possibility that the first cannot be true if the second *or* third is true seems to have been overlooked. In neither case, however, is the objection well taken. For, this would mean that the second and third are in complete conflict, which contradicts the definition he has given of complete conflict of more than two members. The second and third must be in incomplete conflict, which, if affirmed, merely says that the two are not true together, not that they are not false together; therefore, the affirmation of the "second or third" still does not exclude the possibility of the first's being true, while the denial of the first affirms only an incomplete conflict and does not, formally, require that either the second or third is true. Galen seems, in this latter case, to have been trapped by the formalism he decries. For even if three or more propositions are in complete conflict, it is true that any lesser number of them are in incomplete conflict as long as the question of the truth of falsity of each is undetermined. In fact, once the falsity of one has been established, the relation of the others must be complete conflict, and therefore the reasoning could proceed.

Section 5

The treatment here of the first and second indemonstrable seems to be given merely for completeness. It is nevertheless characteristic of Galen's associative way of handling topics. It may be that the source he was following went on to consider the conditionals in relation to consequence and that Galen preferred to reserve the discussion for Chapters XIV and XV. Perhaps he saw that the relation of conditional to consequence was more complicated than the connection of disjunctives and conflict. The discussion of the second indemonstrable does, of course, lead on to the theory of contradiction and conversion which is treated in the next chapter.

CHAPTER VI

Section 1

This sentence contains a grammatical infelicity. Argument and proposition are each singular, connected by "and," and what is rendered "a contradiction of another" is expressed in Greek by *antikeisthai allêlois*, "to contradict each other." It looks at first sight as if Galen is talking about an argument contradicting a proposition or vice versa. In the following sections, however, he first discusses contradictory propositions and then contradictory arguments, so that the translation renders what Galen must mean. Kalbfleisch comments in a note on the passage: "One would expect 'arguments and propositions'."

The connecting of contradiction with complete conflict recalls the passage already quoted from Bekker's *Anecdota* attributing to the Stoics a distinction between conflicting and contradicting.   Since the relation of "conflict" is exactly the relation between contradictories in the square of oppositions, Galen's sentence does no more than assert that contradiction is a special case of conflict.   The Stoic position as given in Bekker stresses the formal distinction, that contradiction is effected by negation.

Section 2

Since section 1 obviously alludes to the fact that contradictories go in pairs, it is clear that the hypothetical propositions mentioned in the first clause of this sentence must be such contradictory pairs.   The section shows the forms that contradictories take for the different kinds of propositions.   The phrase, "exceeds by a negative" (i.e., the word "not") is used by other writers (e.g., Sextus, Alexander), meaning that the negative particle has been added to the sentence to make its contradictory. Presumably Galen has in mind the Stoic practice of negating their "axioms" by prefixing *ouchi* to the whole sentence.

The phrase *apophasei pleonektei* is explained by Sextus (*Adv. Math.*, VIII, 89): (the Stoics) *phasi gar "antikeimena estin hôn to heteron tou heterou apophasei pleonazei."*   Sextus goes on to say that this means that the negative particle is attached to the whole sentence and is not attached to one of the members.

In this treatment of categoricals, Galen combines doctrine derived from the square of oppositions, to take care of universal negative and particular affirmative propositions, with the grammatical point that the negation of "all" serves to introduce a particular negative.   He allows this remark to imply the opposition of universal affirmative and particular negative.   He does not mention here the other form of the particular negative "some are not . . . ."   Following Aristotle's practice, he distinguishes singular propositions from both universal and particular and gives the special form of negation of the singular by simple negation of the predicate.   His example "Socrates is walking" is from a Peripatetic source.   The same example, or the same subject with other verbs, occurs frequently in Alexander.   It is noteworthy here that he does not systematize the doctrine but is content to show how each kind of contradiction may be handled.

Section 3

There are serious textual difficulties in this section.   In the first clause the words "share with" are followed by *tois horois atokias*.   The last word is daggered by Kalbfleisch, who conjectures *tôn horôn allêlais*.

The translation follows this conjecture for want of a better. *Atokia* is cited by L and S only from Musonius. It is possible that Galen is referring to the unfruitfulness of a pair of coterminous sentences.

The doubt about *atokias* is intensified by the confusion at the start of the next clause. The participle *strephousai* agrees with the subject of the clause, but then there is no main verb. Furthermore, *anastrephousai* is required by the sense, since the difference between inversion and conversion is the point of the sentence. Kalbfleisch proposes in his apparatus: *Hôsper ge kai hai anastrephousai te kai antistrephousai: anastrephousi men oun pros. . . .* This makes grammar and sense of the passage; but since Kalbfleisch did not feel justified in printing it in his text, I do not feel justified in translating it. The translation takes the participle as if it were a main verb, for the sake of getting an acceptable English sentence.

The thread of the two sections is that contradictories are pairs of propositions having the same terms but opposite meanings. This brings up the other kind of coterminous pairs in which the order of terms is inverted, and in some cases the inverse proposition remains true if the original is true. Nothing is said here of the partial convertibility of the universal affirmative, although it is made use of later in the reduction of syllogisms to the perfect syllogisms of the first figure. Mau would emend line 13 to introduce partial conversion. Mau also suggests that *synoros* makes its first appearance in this logical sense. In Aristotle it means geographically coterminous.

Section 4

The final clause of this section is not in the MS. but has been supplied by Kalbfleisch. It is a necessary and certain emendation. The example fulfills the definition of converted proposition, being true, if the first is true. Its connection with the second indemonstrable is obvious.

Section 5

In passing from the convertibility of propositions to the convertibility of syllogisms, Galen gives no sign that he is aware that there is a logical difference. By convertible categorical propositions he means any proposition which, when true, gives another true proposition when subject and predicate are interchanged. In other words, conversion of a categorical proposition gives rise to what logicians call an immediate inference, by which knowledge of the truth of one proposition entails knowledge of the truth of another.

In discussing the conversion of hypothetical propositions Galen confines himself to conditionals, probably because he considered the commutativity of the disjunctive not a conversion but merely a rearrangement of terms, in no way affecting the meaning.   Conditionals obviously differ in meaning when the terms are rearranged, as we saw in discussing the last chapter.   Owing to the rule of the contradiction of the consequent, the act of first interchanging the members of a conditional and then negating each produces a second hypothetical "coterminous" with the first and coinciding in truth with it.   In the fact that the members must be negated as well as interchanged, conversion of conditionals combines analogies both to conversion of categoricals and to opposition.

As to the conversion of syllogisms, Galen's rule is the rule of transposition used in the indirect proofs of the moods *Baroco* and *Bocardo* of the categorical syllogisms.   It is set forth by Aristotle in *Prior Analytics* (59 b 3).   The point to be observed here is that Galen's definition now has to be taken in another sense.   The converse of a categorical proposition, being an alternative form of referring to the same state of affairs, the two propositions are true with reference to the same set of facts.   In the case of a converted conditional, the truth of one hypothesis entails the truth of the other, although the relation between the member propositions is contradictory.   But the syllogisms related by transposition are related because the logical validity of the one entails the logical validity of the other.

This statement is subject to a qualification.   If the two syllogisms are expressed in the form of an inference scheme, as is Galen's practice, then the equivalence of the converse syllogisms is merely a matter of logical validity.   If, however, they are expressed in the form of implications, as is usual in Aristotle, then the two sides of the equivalence are true, since each is a true proposition.   The case is then the same as for the conversion of the conditional.   Whether Galen was aware of the distinction between a rule of inference and an implication is not apparent in this book, or, so far as I am aware, elsewhere in Galen.   Galen's statement of the law of transposition suggests the inference scheme form, since he speaks of premisses and conclusions rather than antecedent and consequent. Since Aristotle similarly speaks of premisses and conclusions, this argument is not entirely conclusive.

Aristotle states the law of transposition in discussing conversion of syllogisms.   He uses the same term as Galen, *antistrephein*, and in the sense both of conversion of propositions and of syllogisms.   His treatment of the latter point is much more detailed, apparently for the purpose of providing exercises to increase one's facility with logic.   Galen explicitly excludes exercises from this book, though recommending practice with equivalent forms to anyone who wishes to become skilled in logic, and referring the reader to his other works.

It can be seen, then, that Galen's discussion in this and the preceding sections leans heavily on Aristotle for the doctrine of conversion of categorical propositions and syllogisms. His treatment of conversion of hypotheticals is scanty and seems to be included for completeness. He may have had no treatise on this phase of the subject to refer to and may have been content with showing how the second indemonstrable produced a pair of propositions that satisfied the definition of conversion. In fact, in so far as conversion is thought of as giving an immediate inference, Galen's conversion of hypotheticals is not conversion, since the inference is a product of syllogistic reasoning.

Another way of putting this point is to say that the conversion of a categorical proposition or syllogism is an operation of the logic of terms that requires some of the logic of propositions to validate it, while conversion of hypotheticals is entirely within the logic of propositions. Mau reports the law of contraposition is explicitly formulated by the Stoics as the first thema (Bochenski, *Ancient Formal Logic,* p. 97).

Section 6

Although Galen here sets forth the five indemonstrable hypothetical syllogisms of Chrysippus, this is not his systematic treatment of them. Otherwise, it would be hard to account for the fact that he lists Chrysippus's third, with the negative conjunction as major, without stating his objection to it, as he does so forcefully in both Chapter IV and Chapter XIV. The systematic treatment comes later, in Chapter XIV. The subject of this section is the "modes."

"Modes" (*tropoi*) mean the schematic representation of an argument by means of symbols. In this case the symbols are ordinal numerals and they stand for propositions, as can be seen from the examples of hypothetical propositions already given. Modern symbolic logicians have hailed this Stoic device as an anticipation of their use of symbols as variables. It is not the first use of symbols for variables in expositions of logic. To Aristotle is due that honor. Aristotle's symbols, however, stand for terms. The Stoic symbols stand for propositions, as "p" and "q" and "r" in Russell and Whitehead's *Principia Mathematica*. It is to be noted that Stoic symbolism is incomplete; there are no symbols for the logical constants "if," "or," "and," and "not"; for these the ordinary Greek words are used. This was probably because ancient logicians did not separate logic completely from metaphysics and had no clear conception of a purely logical implication or disjunction. We have already seen how Galen attempts an understanding of disjunction in terms of relations among things about which statements are made, and we know from Diogenes and Sextus that the nature of implication was debated in antiquity; we also learn from their reports that the various positions taken were supported by appeals to factual relations rather than to logical analysis. Following Aristotle's lead it was easier to see that particular terms or propositions were indifferent to the validity of logical forms than that logical relations themselves could be abstracted from material relations of things in the world.

The last clause contains the main point of the section. The long discussion of the modes was a note on the meaning of the term. What Galen asserts in the section is that the syllogistic modes are convertible, just as the syllogisms themselves are. The first and second indemonstrables are related to each other as converses in the sense of section 4. The third, fourth, and fifth, however, each give rise to a converse by interchange of the variables in the minor premiss and the conclusion. This difference is due to the fact, already noted, that in the conditional the terms are not commutative, while in the conjunction and disjunction they are.

Section 7

There is textual difficulty in this section. The words: "or, if one should assume one of the members not to exist" have been supplied by Kalbfleisch. Moreover, the final clause lacks a connective. It could be a gloss, especially since, as it stands, it is a misstatement. The conclusion to the denial of one of the members must be a paradisjunctive not a disjunctive.

Each time Galen treats the five indemonstrables he follows the discussion with a mention of the paradisjunctive. This would seem to indicate that he was familiar with a handling of the five indemonstrables by a scholar who felt that the paradisjunctive had been overlooked by Chrysippus and required notice. His remark in Chapter VI, 1, after defining non-exclusive alteration, that "some name this the paradisjunctive" shows that this form had a kind of appendical relation to traditional handlings of the indemonstrables. The use of the name in a different sense by Gellius shows that the authorities were not all agreed on its meaning.

In any case Galen gives the logically correct forms of syllogism for the paradisjunctive in his sense (that is, if Kalbfleisch's addition is correct). The affirmation of one or more members of a paradisjunctive yields no conclusion about the remaining member, it may be either true or false.

CHAPTER VII
Section 1

Galen's point in calling the major premiss in a hypothetical syllogism determinative of the minor is that the minor premiss is either one of the members of the hypothetical major or its contradictory.

Galen seems to imply that *hegemonikai* is a technical term as well as *tropikon*, which he definitely attributes to Chrysippus. This attribution is confirmed by Alexander (*in Anal. Pr.*, 262, Wallies, 28–30) at least to the extent of being the term of the *neoteroi*, who, in Alexander are always the Stoics and usually Chrysippus and his close followers. Whether the etymology from *tropis* is correct is uncertain. Aristophanes, *Wasps* (30), uses *tropis* metaphorically for the nub of a statement, which suggests a similar point of view. Ps.-Ammonius (*in Anal. Pr.*, Wallies, 68, 6), derives *tropikon* from *tropos*, on the ground that an hypothetical proposition makes a turn from one proposition to another, i.e., is made up of at least two other propositions. This derivation sounds like a guess. Possibly the term should be connected with the "modes." *Hegemonikai* may be used in reference to the Stoic *hegemonikon*, the governing part of the soul of man and the world.

There is a lacuna in the text which Kalbfleisch fills with the words that may be translated, ". . . are there more than two minor premisses, nor in the paradisjunctive." In the present translation Kalbfleisch's paradisjunctive has been altered to "conditional," since it would be strange for one of the principal forms of the indemonstrables to be omitted from this summary. The paradisjunctive, as just pointed out, stands a little aside from the main Chrysippean tradition.

Section 2

The Boethos referred to raises a minor question. There was a Stoic Boethos, an associate of Panaetius; a Peripatetic of the time of Augustus, Boethos of Sidon; and Flavius Boethos, a Roman noble, Galen's early patron, who was a dilettante of Peripatetic philosophy. The only argument in favor of the first is that *hosper kai* might seem to imply that Boethos was not a Peripatetic. But it could single him out from the *tines* of the Peripatetics already mentioned. Flavius Boethos had been dead long before the presumed time of this book. But the mention of the name without qualification as a philosophical authority worthy of respect points to a philosopher rather than a patron of philosophy. The Peripatetic Boethos is known (Pauly-Wissowa sub nomine) to have interested himself in Aristotle's logic and to have had some traces of Stoicism in his thinking. A reference in Ammonius's commentary on the *Prior Analytics* (p. 31, 11, Berlin ed.) makes it practically certain that this Boethos is meant. Ammonius relates that, "Boethos, the eleventh in succession after Aristotle, held contrary to Aristotle, and held rightly and proved, that all the syllogisms in the second and third figures are perfect." This is essentially the same kind of concern that is expressed in Galen's reference to him. Boethos of Sidon, therefore, is the person referred to here.

The controversy over which type of syllogism is primary is reflected in the passage of Alexander already referred to (*in Anal. Pr.*, Wallies, 262ff). Alexander is at pains to vindicate the primacy of the categoricals; he does so by arguing that if the hypotheticals are to yield knowledge, the *proslêpseis* must be true, and since they are categorical propositions, their truth must be established by a categorical syllogism. It is likely, however, that Boethos and the other Peripatetics who held the view quoted had discovered in their analysis of Aristotle's logic that he did, in fact, use hypothetical syllogisms in establishing the validity of the categorical syllogisms. Galen's counterargument, depending as it does on grammatical analysis, would be considered irrelevant by both parties to the dispute; but it does show that Galen sees that Boethos's contention is about a formal question. For this reason, as the next section shows, the question does not interest Galen.

The same passage of Alexander contains a discussion of the term *proslêpsis*, which the Stoics use for the determined minor premiss of an hypothetical syllogism. Alexander reports that the Peripatetics used the term *metalêpsis* for this sort of thing. A *metalêpsis* is a taking of the same thing in a different sense. The minor of a hypothetical is the same as one member of the major (or its contradiction) but is asserted categorically in the minor, but conditionally in the major. A *proslêpsis*, on the other hand, for Peripatetics is the taking of something different into the argument, which, however, had been there potentially. Alexander implies that this shift of terms obscured the dependence of the hypothetical on the categorical syllogisms; for if the minor premiss is asserted categorically, the ground for this assertion is not contained in the hypothetical major and consequently must be established by categorical syllogism or be self-evident. The connotation of change in the *meta* emphasizes this need for additional proof, while *proslêpsis* suggests just the addition of another part to the argument, something that was already there potentially. At any rate, as Alexander says, the Stoic use of *proslêpsis* prevailed.

Section 3

Refusal to take sides in a controversy is characteristic of Galen. If, on the one hand, it shows Galen to be a little blind to the finer issues of logical theory, on the other, it marks him as a man whose sense of the importance of advancing men's positive knowledge in the sciences leads him to shun the rivalries of the philosophical sects. His fundamental outlook is revealed in all his writings: to build a secure science on the tested achievements of any of the schools, to reject any of their opinions which are demonstrably false, and not to engage in futile dispute through mistaken commitment to a preferred school. To be able to demonstrate the truth of an opinion, in medicine as in any other field of knowledge, is the aim of the scientist. The value of any logical form lies in its usefulness for demonstration, not in its conformity to a particular theory of the nature of logic.

Section 4

This section lacks lucidity. The main point is clear; in the indemonstrable hypotheticals the minor premiss is a verbatim repetition of part of the major premiss and introduces no new term or proposition; on the other hand, the minor premiss of a categorical carries over one term of the major, but introduces a new term, which may be almost anything the speaker pleases (so long as it is within the proper universe of discourse), and may be affirmative or negative in a variety of ways. It may be suggested that the disjunction of affirmative and negative is a parenthesis within the major disjunction of carrying over the whole or part of the major, and that it thus makes a cross classification of possible minor premisses.

Section 5

In the text the conclusions of the two illustrative syllogisms are omitted and supplied by Kalbfleisch. "Of these terms" follows Orth's translation of the corrupt *tôn erôntôn*; presumably Orth proposed to read: *tôn horôn tônd*, a reasonable conjecture.

Galen disregards the question as to whether the additional premiss turns up as major or minor in his finished syllogism. Perhaps he means in this way to illustrate the greater freedom of choice in the categorical syllogisms. He has not yet introduced the schemata of the valid categorical syllogisms and is interested only in illustrating the point of the preceding section. He does not arrange his premisses in the order major-minor, revealing once more his prejudice against the fussiness of formality.

Mau refers to Prantl in marking the difference between Aristotle and Galen: Aristotle has a conclusion and seeks a middle term. Galen starts with major premiss and suggests various minor premisses.

Section 6

Most of the last few lines of the section are an addition of Kalbfleisch's. They are necessary, because, as the next section shows, Galen is illustrating the Aristotelian figures here and without the additions the illustration is truncated beyond recognition.

Galen uses the name "common term" for the middle term of the categorical syllogism. He introduces it without definition, since it is obvious from the examples.

Mau comments that Kalbfleisch need not have filled in the conclusions of the illustrative syllogisms, since the text is concerned only with the arrangement of terms in the premises.

Sections 7, 8, 9

The terms used in the examples illustrating the three Aristotelian figures are stock terms, found already in Aristotle's *Topics*. They may reflect, too, the Stoic concentration on ethical questions. Since Galen will not be demonstrating the validity of the valid syllogisms, he does not use the varied and carefully chosen terms that Aristotle uses in the *Prior Analytics*.

CHAPTER VIII

Sections 1, 2

Galen does not speak of "moods" in the three figures, but of "syllogisms." Any actual syllogism will have the form of one and one mood only of one of the three figures. The figures are, thus, generic and the syllogisms specific differentiae. The term "syllogism" here names a specific thing, not the reasoning process or the generic form. Galen follows Aristotle's practice in speaking of the "syllogisms" in the different figures.

Aristotle does not call the syllogisms of the first figure "indemonstrable," but "perfect" (*teleios*). The imperfect syllogisms are "reduced" (*anagein*) to those of the first figure, not demonstrated from them. Probably this is because, for Aristotle, demonstration is carried out with syllogisms, deriving knowledge from necessary and true premises. The reduction of syllogisms makes use, informally in Aristotle, of the propositional logic and so would not be demonstration in his sense. When Chrysippus had extended the meaning of demonstration to include the propositional logic, he could call his primary syllogisms "indemonstrable," and Galen, in turn, could use the term of the categoricals of the first figure.

The remark that Chrysippus's second indemonstrable requires demonstration is puzzling. The point is, as Galen has already in effect shown, the conversion of "if the first, then the second," to "if not the second, then not the first," makes the second indemonstrable a derivative of the first.

Section 3

Having described the arrangement of terms in the three figures, in section 7 of the preceding chapter, Galen feels no need to repeat himself here, and so there is no mention of the common term. The succinctness of the language and the accurate reproduction of the Aristotelian order suggest a school text or syllabus, such as must have been used in the Peripatetic schools, or perhaps generally in the common schools. The moods are described rather than defined, and the Aristotelian symbolism is abandoned. The moods, of course, are the familiar *Barbara, Celarent, Darii Ferio*. Galen cannot resist one etymology, *symperasma*, defined as if spatially beyond the premises.

CHAPTER IX

Sections 1, 2, 3

Why Galen, in section 3, restricts this reduction to "some persons" is not clear, since the reduction is particularly easy and is given by Aristotle (*Anal. Pr.*, 27 a 53ff). Kalbfleisch conjectures that the statement was preceded by a clause (which dropped out) asserting that some persons reduce this mood by reduction *per impossibile*. Since in *Prior Analytics*, Aristotle first considers *Festino* and *Baroco* together as having one universal and one particular premiss and then discusses them separately according as the major or minor is affirmative or negative, and since *Baroco* is reduced *per impossibile*, this may account for such an omitted clause.

Sections 4, 5

Galen follows the Aristotelian way of reducing *Baroco* to *Barbara*. He uses the Stoic device of ordinal numerals to represent the terms in the premisses and conclusion, instead of Aristotle's letters. His explanation is more detailed than Aristotle's. The latter says: "If M belongs to all N, but not to some X, necessarily N does not belong to some X; for if it belongs to all, and M is predicated of all N, necessarily M belongs to all X; but by hypothesis it does not belong to some" (*Anal. Pr.*, 27 a 37ff).

Most of Galen's statement is an amplification of Aristotle's. His last clause, however, is an expression of what Aristotle leaves to the reader's understanding, and it goes slightly off the point, since the correct conclusion is that the second is not predicated of some of the third. It is possible that an *ou* has dropped out.

Of course, Galen may have written the text as it stands, and meant that the second is not predicated of all, but if any, just of some, and hence that there is some that it is not predicated of. He seems not to have been content to rely on the reader's remembering that he has already shown that the universal affirmative is the contradictory of the particular negative, though he has used that opposition in the body of the proof.

Both Aristotle (*Anal. Pr.*, 59 3) and Galen knew the law of transposition, which establishes the validity of *Baroco* from *Barbara*, without raising the question of the truth of the premisses in either syllogism. Aristotle may have avoided the use of this law because he had not developed ways of handling the logic of propositions and felt that his method was clearer or more immediately evident. Galen follows him willingly, because he prefers to go beyond the verbal forms to the world of things, as we have seen many times already. However, as Lukasiewicz has pointed out (*Aristotle's Syllogistic*, p. 55), the Aristotelian reduction works only when the premisses are true, and hence is not valid generally for all premisses.

Section 6

By exposition the conclusion of *Baroco* is drawn from a syllogism in *Casare* or *Camestres*; it is uncertain which Galen means, since he is not careful to state his premisses always in the same order. Since both these syllogisms have already been reduced to the first figure, this establishes the validity of *Baroco*. The method of taking a part of the extension of the minor term and constructing a universal proposition with it as subject has been shown by Lukasiewicz to be equivalent to the symbolic logician's use of existential quantifiers. "*There is* a part of the third, none of which has the first predicated of it."

CHAPTER X

Section 1

The words "particular affirmative" before "conclusion" are missing in the MS. text and added by Kalbfleisch. They are necessary to the sense and must have been written by Galen.

No mention of partial conversion occurs in the section Galen devotes to conversion of categorical propositions. There, Galen was interested in the production by conversion of propositions that were equivalent, in the sense of being true together and having the same quality. Here he uses the word conversion without qualification, but his correct reference to the mood *Darii* shows that he understood it as partial conversion. Perhaps a statement about partial conversion has fallen out of the earlier passage. Mau, commenting on that passage, conjectures that to be the case.

Sections 2, 3

In section 3 Galen, as usual, makes no mention of transposition of premisses, since he is unconcerned with their order.

Some words in the translation are not in Kalbfleisch's text, but he notes in his apparatus that he suspects they have fallen out of the text. They have been translated since they are necessary to the sense.

There is, furthermore, a textual difficulty. The last clause reads *apo tês en merei antistrapheisês kai proseti tou symperasmatos*; Kalbfleisch daggers *apo*. Omitting this leaves a genitive absolute, which makes sense on the assumption that Galen expects the reader by this time to understand that he is giving the mechanics of conversion. It may be that a corrector at some point felt a preposition was needed, though one would have thought he would have supplied *dia* from the last clause.

Section 4

Here, too, the mood to which this syllogism is converted is not mentioned, and the mechanics are expressed by a genitive absolute. The words, "and a particular affirmative," are added by Kalbfleisch.

In the last clause the term "minor premiss" stands that way in the text. Previously, where the translation reads "minor premiss," Galen has written "the premiss at the minor term." As Galen proceeds through his catalogue of forms, he is willing to adopt terminological shortcuts.

Section 5

With this mood Galen departs from Aristotle's order of presentation for the first time. The same transposition of moods of the third figure occurs in ps-Apuleius's *peri hermêneias*, suggesting a common tradition for Galen and the latter. (Mau suggests it goes back to Theophrastus.) The significance of the change of order seems to be a desire to keep parallel with the second figure and a feeling that the special nature of the reduction of *Bocardo* put it more properly at the end.

Sections 6, 7, 8

These sections discuss the mood *Bocardo* and the two methods of reduction, *per impossibile* and by exposition, in a manner exactly parallel to the treatment of *Baroco* at the end of the last chapter. The final conclusion of the reduction in a particular negative is this time correctly stated.

CHAPTER XI

Section 1

I have translated *adokimoi* by "invalid," both because this is the term commonly used in traditional logic for such combinations of premisses and because Plato in *Laws* (742a) uses the word of the internal currency of his state, which "though *entimon* to the citizens is *adokimon* to other men"; furthermore, Alexander, commenting on *Topics* (162 b 4, Wallies, 576, 14) which discusses the various meanings of false *logos*, says that the argument *per impossibile* uses false *logoi*, but is not *adokimon*.

The second clause of the section, mentioning the distinction first made in Aristotle's *Topics* between dialectical and apodictic or scientific syllogisms, is put in to make clear that the traditionally conceived lesser certainty of dialectic is not due to its use of less rigorous arguments and hence it does not use the invalid moods, that is, it is not sophistical. Mau corrects "dialectically" to "through indication," plausibly, but my argument here may be correct. The following clause connects *endeixis* with dialectic through one of Galen's terminological notes. The definition of *endeixis* is hard to translate. Its connection with dialectic lies in its being a "finding of the thing sought"; this "finding" is "from the nature of the thing" *ek tês tou pragmatos phuseos* and "*according to things clearly apparent.*" The key to understanding is in the phrase *enargôs phainomena*. In his medical works Galen finds fault over and over again with doctrinaire physicians who refuse to accept the clearly apparent as starting point and guide to further knowledge. In *The Natural Faculties*, for instance, the physiologist is shown to work from the clearly apparent facts of digestion to the discovery of the assimilative and other faculties. These are, no doubt, what he has in mind in speaking of the nature of the thing. It is with this kind of reasoning that *endeixis* is concerned. The term is a medical term and is preserved in the modern medical use of the word "indication." The Stoics and Epicureans talked much about indicative signs, by which they meant such things as that a woman's giving milk was a sign that she had conceived, or that a scar was a sign that a man had been wounded. In these discussions the relation of sign and fact was often expressed in a conditional sentence, but it could also be expressed in a categorical form.

> Major premiss: those who are scarred have been wounded.
> Minor premiss: Dion has scars.
> Conclusion: Dion has been wounded.

On this interpretation the *enargôs phainomena* would be stated in the minor premiss, the "nature of the fact" in the major premiss, and the "finding of the thing sought" in the conclusion. Such an argument would be dialectical in the Aristotelian sense, because most major premises of this sort would not be apodictically known but would be what Aristotle calls *endoxa*. To revert to medicine, "informed (or authoritative) medical opinion" would be one of the things Aristotle considered *endoxa*. So in all the affairs of life, there are areas where the major premises of arguments must be "informed opinion" and the minor, "things clearly apparent." Serious searchers for truth in such affairs would use valid syllogisms, just as apodictic scientists would, but their conclusions would be dialectical rather than scientific.

A way to understand Galen's definition of *endeixis*, then, is that an investigator follows the clues given by things clearly apparent, to derive an understanding of the thing sought from the relation between the clue and what it signifies, which is a relation given by nature and open to him who can form his opinion from the study of nature.

Section 2

Although Galen has excluded discussion of the invalid combinations of premises, he is aware of the arithmetical combinations that yield forms of syllogisms to be tested for validity, and again recommends exercises to the student. Not only are there the sixteen possible combinations in each figure, but the existence of alternative forms of expression of the premises increases the number of exercises for the student to practice on. He refers here to an authentic work of his, *On Equivalent Propositions*, a title we know from his *De Libris Propriis*. By form of expression he means, for instance, that the particular negative can be expressed either in the form, "Not all A is B," or in the form, "Some A is not B." He does not share the modern logician's concern to restrict logical statements to one form.

It is noteworthy that when he calls the present work an "outline of logical theory," the Greek for "logical" is *logikês*. This adjective is rarely the equivalent of the modern "logical." In Aristotle it usually means something like "abstract" or "verbal," while in the traditional and Stoic partition of philosophy into physics, ethics, and logic, it means the whole range of linguistics, epistemology, and logic in the modern sense.

Sections 3 through 7

What Galen means is that a syllogism that has a universal affirmative as its conclusion may also conclude the corresponding particular affirmative, which follows by immediate inference from the universal. Furthermore, this particular affirmative, being simply convertible, its converse also follows from the premises of the original syllogism. A particular negative follows from a universal negative conclusion, but since it is not convertible, nothing further follows.

The discussion begun in this section continues through the rest of the chapter. The text is uncertain in section 4, but what we have is a listing of valid conclusions that can be drawn, by conversions of conclusions and transpositions of premisses, that are different from those directly attainable from the fourteen valid moods.

In section 3 mention is made of the particular conclusions that can be drawn from the universal conclusions directly obtained from universal premisses. Then the further conclusion is obtained by converting the particular affirmative already drawn. This would cover the first mood of the fourth figure, or the first mood of the first indirect figure, where a particular affirmative with major as subject and minor as predicate by conversion yields a conclusion in the standard form.

In section 4 the statement is made that the first two moods of the first figure yield universal conclusions, affirmative and negative respectively, which include the particulars of the same quality. The lacuna probably contained reference to the indirect moods, which yield a universal negative and a particular affirmative by conversion to get major and minor terms in the right order.

In section 5 the device of transposing premisses to get a valid syllogism from an invalid combination of premisses is stated. It is then illustrated in section 6 with the cases of the last two indirect (or fourth figure moods), where the invalid combinations of an affirmative major premiss (universal or particular) with a universal negative in the first figure are validated by transposing premisses, concluding the minor predicated of the major in a particular negative.

Section 7 points out that the first and second of the second figure, and the third and fourth of the third, are related by the fact that they both may transpose their premisses and convert their conclusions to show that they stand in a reciprocal relation to each other.

The chief interest of these sections is their connection with the so-called Galenic fourth figure of the syllogism. The fourth figure is the one in which the middle term is predicate in the major premiss and subject in the minor, making then a pattern the reverse of the first figure. It was known to the Middle Ages and to modern times but is unknown in antiquity. There is no mention of it, as a separate figure, in any work of Galen's. The story that he invented it is derived from a few obscure notices in Arab writers or in sources derived from the Arabic (see Lukasiewicz, *Aristotle's Syllogistic*, pp. 38–42). The logic of the fourth figure was handled by Aristotle and Theophrastus in what was known as the indirect first figure. This is the doctrine of these sections of the present work. There is no justification for attributing the invention of the fourth figure to Galen.

Mau has many suggested emendations in this difficult chapter, which commend themselves to the judicious commentator. He agrees that the moods of the so-called fourth figure are involved here and some of his emendations bring explicit mention of them.

CHAPTER XII

Section 1

Galen has not said anywhere previously that these syllogisms are called categorical. In Chapter VII, 9, he defined categorical premises or propositions, pointing out that, although categorical means affirmative, the term had been consecrated by usage to apply to both affirmative and negative propositions consisting of a single predication. In the first section of Chapter VIII he speaks of syllogisms that occur in the three figures among the categorical premises. This is sufficient authorization for the transfer of the adjective from the proposition to the syllogism.

All the instances of *katêgorikos* and its adverb listed in Bonitz's index to Aristotle have the sense "affirmative." The verb *katêgoreô* is used by Aristotle commonly in the sense "to predicate." There was no need for the present sense of "categorical" until the hypothetical propositions and syllogisms had been elaborated by the Stoics. In Sextus and Alexander the technical sense of categorical as opposed to hypothetical is clearly established.

Galen implies in the last clause of this section that this meaning of categorical was derived from the "categories"; this seems hardly likely. It seems rather that it derived from the generalization of the term predicative to include both affirmative and negative predication, possible since the verb was already used in this general sense and Aristotle supplied the term *kataphatikon* to cover the restricted sense of "affirmative." From this sense, applied to the proposition, its transfer to the syllogism followed, as Galen correctly indicates.

Galen's mistaken belief about the etymology of the word categorical leads to his notion of the rather mechanical use of these syllogisms for the investigation of questions falling under the various categories. His omission of the category of substance from those in which the categorical syllogisms are useful is something else again. As will be seen, it comes from his belief that questions of substance can be dealt with by hypothetical syllogisms. This view, in turn, stems from a metaphysical position, which it is doubtful that Galen has thought through. He probably is reflecting a traditional teaching of the generations immediately before him.

To return to the use of the categorical syllogisms, since the way Aristotle, in the *Posterior Analytics*, conceives their use does have them showing the possession of a predicate by a subject through a middle term, and since, for Aristotle, all predicates fall under one or another of the categories, Galen's statement is not so much incorrect as misleading. He has erected into a principle what is in effect a necessary concomitant of Aristotle's analysis. Galen's illustrations in this chapter are, therefore, a labored series of examples which prove nothing in particular. They are, however, not without interest, for they are examples of the kind of questions that the science of the day was interested in. They provide additional detail in the picture that emerged from his first treatment of the categories in Chapter II.

Section 2

According to Heath, *Aristarchus of Samos* (Oxford, 1913, pp. 339-40), Eratosthenes is reported to have determined the length of the earth's circumference as either 250,000 stadia or 252,000. The accounts report that Eratosthenes knew that the sun at equinox cast no shadow at noon in Syene, roughly 5,000 stadia from Alexandria, and, so he believed, on the same meridian; at Alexandria it cast a shadow in a bowl equal to one-fiftieth of a circle. These data give 250,000 stadia. What led to the corrected figure, if such it is, is unknown.

Galen does not tell us what the categorical syllogisms were by which these data yielded Eratosthenes's conclusion. It would seem that they are syllogisms of the type dealt with in Chapter XVIII: relational syllogisms of proportion. Since Galen says that relational syllogisms can be reduced to categorical, though with some violence, he probably felt that it was unnecessary to explain precisely how they were constructed.

The similar questions that follow are evidence of progress made in scientific geography. Mau attributes them to Eratosthenes. Galen mentions no estimates of sizes, or names of students of the subject, possibly indicating that the questions were still unanswered. It may be, however, that the pioneer work of Eratosthenes was so famous as to call for the mention of his name, while the later work was more in the nature of working on already beaten paths. The questions are of interest to the historian of science as evidence of a continued study of the earth and the mapping out of its regions.

Ptolemy's *Geography*, Bk. 1, describes the method of computing the length of the circumference of the earth and discusses methods of determining latitude and longitude, as well as delimiting the extent of the inhabited zones of the earth. Galen's references are too general to show correspondence with Ptolemy's work, but he and Galen were near contemporaries. Galen no doubt knew of Ptolemy's interests through friends that frequented the Temple of Peace, the intellectual center in

Rome at that time (cf. *De Libris Propriis*, Kuehn, XIX, 21: devotees of *technai logikai* gather there).

The last clause of the section is difficult to interpret. The translation given: "and what fraction of each of the inhabited zones is the part above the arctic circle" is very uncertain. The Greek reads *to te ex arktou to hypoloipon [hos]ôn esti moriôn ekastêi tôn oikeseôn*. First, it is a question as to whether "the part remaining from the Arctic Circle" refers to the zone above the circle or below it. Then the dative *hekastêi* is hard to understand in relation to the measuring term, "of how many parts." Finally, the mention of "each of the inhabited zones" suggests either that Arctic stands compendiously for "Arctic and Antarctic" or that reference to the Antarctic has fallen out. Mau seems to refer this to elevation of the celestial north pole. This would make sense of *hekastêi*.

In answer to the first question, the use of *ex*, together with the fact that the connotation suggests that the Arctic and Antarctic Circles are thought of as bounding the inhabited zones, makes it more probable that the reference is to the lands above the circle. The second question may be answered by saying that the dative is a dative of the possessor, "of how many parts belonging to each of . . ."; this is awkward, but the expression of fractional measurements is always somewhat awkward in Greek. In the third question, the "each" does suggest that the Antarctic must be understood as coming into consideration. Regardless of the difficulties of the sentence, it seems that the meaning is roughly as translated.

Section 3

The perfect tenses show that these problems had been solved. This and the preceding section breathe a spirit of pride in the achievements of modern science in Galen's enlightened age. The examples given in this section and in the first part of the next testify to the working out in detail of these scientific questions. The leads given by Eratosthenes, Archimedes, Aristarchus, and others bore many fruits in the work of Alexandrian investigators. The reference in section 4 to the use of water clocks and sundials shows the progress in engineering as well as in theoretical science that characterized the age. The generality with which Galen refers to these activities precludes finding an exact date to which they may be referred. On the whole, the types of studies suggest an age of exploration of the use of new methods and devices rather than the systematizing theoretical work of a Ptolemy. It may be conjectured that Galen's information comes from Posidonius's encyclopedic gatherings of knowledge which summed up the achievements of the Alexandrians and others of the second century B.C.

Section 4

There is a difficulty about the word "star" in this section. The sizes and distance of stars do not seem to have been objects of investigation to the ancients. Probably the word should be "moon" and the reference is to the work of Aristarchus. Mau finds the section corrupt, but his commentary and translation seem to me not very lucid.

The clause beginning "and in sum . . ." contains a clause introduced by the interrogative pronoun *tines*, a correction from the indefinite of the MS.

It is possible, however, that Galen had let himself be carried away by his recital of the achievements of science, and in this part of the section he is recalling that he was really concerned with illustrating how the categorical syllogisms are useful for scientific work. The clauses discussed may be his way of making a transition back to his theme. Read this way, what he says is that the methods that study such quantitative problems use categorical syllogisms. The last clause then states that the enunciations of the findings of the scientists are all expressed in universal propositions.

Mau points out a passage in Galen's *Diagnosis and Treatment of Mental Diseases* (Kuehn, V, 68) in which there is a similar reference to measuring instruments, such as is made here.

Sections 5, 6

The mention of universal propositions at the end of the last section leads to another of Galen's footnotes. This time he takes up the question of greater and less universality. He points out that a proposition about a more restricted subject, such as an isosceles triangle, as compared with a triangle in general, may still be universal if the predication is one that applies to all isosceles triangles and none that are not. Aristotle's *Posterior Analytics* (85 b) discusses this question with an example of an isosceles triangle.

Sections 7, 8, 9

Finally, Galen appends a further note on the verbal expression of universal propositions. He calls attention to the use of the generic article as equivalent to the universal quantifier, showing further that it may be either plural or even singular. He bases the use of the singular generic article on the fact that a noun may stand for the species as well as the individual. Finally, he has an Aristotelian note on species, which is one in nature but in existence is as many as the individuals in its extension. Here he states the modern distinction between class and class concept.

CHAPTER XIII

Section 1

Although in Chapter XII there is no mention of the category of substance, the syllogism in *Barbara* that is offered here in illustration of the double form of expression is one in which the predicates belong to that category; in fact, the major term is the word *ousia* itself. Too much cannot be made of the point, however, since the example is a stock one and Galen's attention is still on the question of variant forms of expression of the universal, which he had begun in the last sections of the preceding chapter.

In the beginning of Chapter II Galen split the category of substance in two, his first example had to do with simple existence and his second with substance in the sense of a composite. His example, it will be recalled, was "Air is a body." It looks as if the word *ousia* has begun by this time to have something of the connotation of the modern "substance" rather than the Aristotelian metaphysical complexity.

Galen has particular difficulty in keeping this chapter in focus. It begins with a discussion of the different usefulness of the moods of the syllogism, but it slides back into the relation of the categorical syllogisms to the categories. In this section, the pre-eminence of the first figure for scientific demonstrations, a dogma since Aristotle, is affirmed. Probably the example chosen put Galen's mind back on the relation to the categories.

Galen does not mention Aristotle's requirement that apodictic science use syllogisms with necessary premisses. It is possible that Aristotle's idea of necessary propositions was too unclear for working scientists such as Galen. Alexander has much to say about necessary propositions and syllogisms from necessary premisses, but he is writing a commentary on the *Prior Analytics* and has them to deal with directly. Galen means essentially the same thing as Aristotle by scientific demonstration, but he is concerned with the universality of the scientific matter, taking for granted its necessity. Galen does not differ from Aristotle in founding demonstrative knowledge on self-evident truth. This is clear from Chapter I, as well as from many passages in his other works.

It is to be noted that Galen has no more qualms than Aristotle about stating the minor premiss first in a syllogism. He would not understand Prantl or Maritain, who consider it a sin to begin a syllogism with anything but the major premiss.

Sections 2, 3, 4

Perhaps in section 3 Galen means by "enunciations" (*apophanseis*) the proved statement of some fact that cannot be considered a fully scientific statement because it is not universal, but that may have some usefulness in systematizing knowledge.

There is something wrong in the example in section 4, since it demonstrates a universal negative (if Kalbfleisch's supplementation is right, as it must be). What Galen seems to mean is that particular affirmatives occur only in figures 1 and 3, while negatives occur in all three figures.

Section 5

"Taken for demonstration" means taken as a subject of which something is to be demonstrated.

The "more indefinite" statements turn out to be the two forms of particular propositions. The exemplification of a syllogism with a particular negative conclusion, which was promised in the preceding section, is found here. Mau comments that at end of 4 Camestres is given; 5 shows this generalized to *Baroco*.

Sections 6 through 10

Galen now returns to listing propositions demonstrated in each of the categories. In the preceding chapter, he says, the syllogisms were all demonstrating things in the category of quantity. It may be that the order was planned, but the text gives the appearance of an afterthought. The examples of syllogisms about pleasure and choice remind him that the category they demonstrate is quality. Therefore he goes on through the list. Again, as in Chapter II, the subjects used as examples range over the encyclopedia of the times: ethical problems for quality, the *pons asinorum* of Euclid for relation, the location of the earth for place, the dates of Hippocrates and Democritus for time, quality again for the sphericity of the earth. Action and passion are the categories under which cause is investigated, several medical questions and several in "philosophy" which turn out to be physics or natural philosophy. Wealth and poverty are placed in the category of state, and a new category of "composition" with weaving and plaiting as examples is given. Finally, position is illustrated with surgical questions.

This list, like the former one, includes questions that began to be studied in the late fifth century B.C., e.g., the location of the earth in the center of the cosmos, or the sphericity of the earth, and continued to be developed through the first century B.C. With the exception of the last two, there is nothing that need be any later than that. The question as to the relative dates of Democritus and Hippocrates calls to mind the Alexandrian studies in chronology. The questions about the causes of voice, respiration, nourishment, and digestion, while they are medical topics that were dealt with by Galen himself, were also the subjects of study by medical men from the fourth century onward. As can be seen from Lucretius, they were debated between the Epicureans and the Stoics, and settled opinions in both schools, as well as in more purely medical circles, existed by the end of the second century. The questions about earthquakes and thunder and lightning that are assigned to "philosophy" are met in the pseudo-Galenic *History of Philosophy*, (Kuehn, XIX) which is generally supposed to be derived from the doxographical work of Aëtius, who wrote in the time of Augustus.

As far as the content of these examples goes, there is nothing to suggest that the whole group may not have been taken over en masse from a source descending from the first century B.C., unless the reference to Hippocrates and the greater number of medical examples under action and passion can be taken to indicate that Galen compiled the list for himself, or at least revised it to include more of his special interests. If it is a traditional list, then it is a question whether it originally served the purpose it does here to exemplify the kind of subjects studied by means of categorical syllogisms. This raises the further question of how the identification of categorical syllogisms with the categories began. Obviously it must have been later than Chrysippus and it cannot have been earlier than the revival of Aristotelian studies in the first century B.C., since, after Chrysippus, apparently, little attention was paid to Aristotelian logic before the first century. The connection is not the invention of Galen, who would in that case have made a definite statement in his best etymological vein, instead of taking their relation for granted. Pending further investigation, it may be suggested that the scheme somehow emanates from the school of Posidonius.

Sections 11, 12

With these two sections the list of categorical subjects closes, but the last two members of the list stand on a different footing from the others. Galen claims as his original discovery a new category of "composition," while the examples of studies under the category of position speak with the authentic voice of a medical practitioner, or, because of the piety towards Hippocrates, of Galen himself.

With regard to composition, Galen's statement at first leads one to suppose that he would put the compositor in his new category, but it seems more likely that he is thinking rather of the composite thing. This is distinguished from simple things, or things whose composition is disregarded, situated in certain places, postures, or states. No doubt his anatomical experience, perhaps his idea of the assimilative faculty in the body and its product, suggested the independence and usefulness of this category.   Aristotle had discussed mixture and composition as a problem in physics, especially difficult for a non-atomic physicist.   From this discussion Galen may have got his idea for the category.   It is unlikely that it would have met with Aristotle's approval.   For him, it would be a confusion of part-and-whole with matter-and-form.

The discussion of the category of position, by means of examples of medical treatment is not only a refreshing improvement on Aristotle's flat "sitting" and "lying," but it also suggests how syllogistic reasoning might apply to the category through consideration of what is the best position for the setting of a broken leg, or for stopping the flow of blood from a wound.

Mau comments on "composition" that Simplicius, commenting on Aristotle's *Categories* (1 b 25, 60–75, Kalbfleisch), reviews the literature on categories and mentions neither Galen nor "composition."   This suggests to Mau that the category began and ended its career here.

CHAPTER XIV

Section 1

In this chapter Galen turns from the categorical syllogisms to the formal exposition of the hypotheticals.   Since he has twice anticipated discussion of them, in connection with conversion and with the so-called "modes," much of the material is repetitious.

This first section distinguishes the hypotheticals from the categoricals in terms of their use.   While the categoricals, according to Galen, demonstrate within all the categories except the first in his listing in Chapter II, the hypotheticals are useful for demonstrating the existence of what is not visibly evident.   The examples given are traditional theses debated in the schools of philosophy.   The first two are Stoic affirmations, the last Epicurean.   No doubt they were in Galen's time the common property of educated men.

Galen does not say that the hypotheticals are exclusively used in questions of this sort.   In Chapter XVI, in fact, he discusses a relational argument and casts it in both categorical and hypothetical form.   Moreover, in *De Semine* (Kuehn, IV, 609), Galen argues in support of a certain opinion by means both of a hypothetical and a categorical syllogism. What the present passage implies is that in arguing for the existence of an ultimate, such as Fate or the void, one must proceed hypothetically, since there can be no higher principle from which to argue categorically. This consideration supports the interpretation given of the difficult definition of *endeixis* in Chapter XI, 1.

Section 2

Galen has already described these propositions in Chapter III and has given the Peripatetic and Stoic terminology. In the last clause *sumphôneitai autois* though impersonal in construction, expresses Galen's acceptance of the validity of the hypothetical syllogisms based on the conditional and the disjunctive. He expresses this agreement to prepare for his rejection of the third indemonstrable as Chrysippus conceived it, which follows in the next section.

Possibly the statement of agreement is meant more widely. It could mean that the tradition of logical doctrine accepts these syllogisms unanimously, but that there was substantial objection to the negative conjunction. As has been seen, Cicero's handling of that syllogism, in his *Topics*, indicates a variation in the traditional way of teaching it.

Section 3

Here Galen restates his rejection of the syllogism founded on the negative conjunctive and couples with it the rejection of any syllogisms in the Stoic sense beyond the five indemonstrables. Since Galen refers to other places for his proof of the invalidity of this syllogism, the apparent difficulties involved in this and the following sections are due to the cursory nature of his reference. One problem is raised by the fact that in the next chapter he will discuss two syllogisms founded on the para-disjunctive. It is possible that Galen means that the Stoics did not recognize more than the five indemonstrables, although others were proposed, or, possibly, these two syllogisms are not indemonstrable. His main point, however, is the rejection of the form of the third indemonstrable as given by Chrysippus. The mention of other syllogisms to be rejected is incidental, occurring by the kind of association of ideas which has already been seen in this work. The last clause is another which indicates the scope and purpose of this book.

Section 4

This section is confused by a serious corruption of the text. After the major premiss, "Dion is not both . . . etc." no more of the syllogism occurs but the words "*kai toude paidion,*" followed by the assertion "to be useful for demonstration, etc." The translation leaves the lacuna in the text, omitting the corrupt words. As things stand, the section has no main verb.

Kalbfleisch suggests in his note that the lacuna was filled with the words: "but he is at Athens, therefore he is not on the Isthmus; and we have demonstrated this . . . ," making this the subject of the following "to be useful for demonstration." This correction is probably right, but it has been left out of the translation because the sense of the whole section is rather obscure and Kalbfleisch's correction amounts to an interpretation.

In order to divine the sense, one must first see that the beginning of the section asserts that the followers of Chrysippus believe that the third indemonstrable is founded on a negative conjunctive as major; Galen, we know, denies this. He goes on, however, to assert that the form exemplified in the well-known "Dion not at Athens and the Isthmus at once" is useful for demonstration. The grounds for this assertion follow in the next sections. How Galen made clear the connection between his two assertions is hidden in the lost portion of the text. Kalbfleisch's conjecture does not seem to make it sufficiently clear, and so it has been omitted.

Sections 5, 6

Galen is now in a position to make his stand in opposition to Chrysippus clear. He repeats his distinction between complete and incomplete conflict. The syllogism in question is useful for demonstration when its major premiss refers to a situation of incomplete conflict between facts. Chrysippus's formulation of the syllogism is satisfactory, but he has failed to see that the formulation may be interpreted differently in different situations.

Sections 7, 8

To clarify further this difference, Galen restates the three kinds of logical combination of clauses in a proposition: conflict, consequence, and conjunction. To achieve balance he states the case of consequence inaccurately. While it is true that both complete and incomplete conflict express relations between facts that are never true together, complete consequence does express the condition of always being true together, but incomplete conflict, as the next chapter makes clear, expresses facts that are never false together and may be true together. Conjunction, in Galen's view, expresses a combination of facts in which there is no necessity of their being true (or false) together. It is true that a conjunction is not a true statement unless both the members are true, but this is not what Galen is concerned with. Even when the conjunction is true, the connection between the facts stated in the member clauses is fortuitous.

Galen says in section 8 that from a denial of a conjunction and the assertion of one of its members the denial of the other member does follow, but he denies that such a form of argument is useful for demonstration.   Possibly the explanation of why this is so had been given in the *De Demonstratione*.   It is only reasonable to suppose that the denial of two unrelated facts conjoined is not a situation likely to be met by an anatomist or a physiologist who is interested in natural connections or repugnancies among things.

Sections 9, 10, 11

After apologizing for this digression—it is interesting to find Galen aware of this besetting sin—he returns to his topic and concludes the chapter by listing the hypothetical syllogisms as he accepts them.   He keeps the numbering of Chrysippus and points out that his third form is to be understood in the sense of incomplete conflict and not as Chrysippus had presented it as a denied conjunction.

The trouble Galen has taken with the difference between his form of the third indemonstrable and Chrysippus's indicates that he is working up new material, possibly his own, rather than transmitting established doctrine.

CHAPTER XV

Sections 1, 2

When Galen presented the paradisjunctive in Chapter V, 1, he did not say that it expressed incomplete consequence.   In fact, this is the first mention of incomplete consequence in the book.   He said there, and repeats here, that one member of the proposition must be true and that one, or more than one, or all of the other members may be true.   This is the non-exclusive disjunctive or alternation of modern logic.   It is properly called incomplete consequence since all may be true together, where in incomplete conflict all may be false together.   In the case of the complete forms of consequence and conflict, complete conflict requires that one member be true and the other or others false, while complete consequence requires that both (or all) must be true or both (or all) false. Stakelum pointed this out to show that Galen's theory admitted the biconditional or equivalence of modern logic.   Since this leaves out of account the conditional or implication, in which, if the first is true, the second must be true, while, if the first is false, the second may be either true or false, there is a gap in Galen's analysis of hypothetical propositions in terms of consequence and conflict.   The conditional is all that is needed for the first and second indemonstrables, and it is what is signified by the Greek particle *ei*, which Galen uses as the sign of the synemmenon. The difference between the commutative disjunction and the non-commutative conditional has already been pointed out.   Galen's theory has a neatness about it, but it leaves some aspects of hypothetical propositions unaccounted for.

Section 3

Galen's example is typical of subjects that are treated in his technical medical works.   He may have elaborated the paradisjunctive because reflection on his own practice showed him that it often was useful, and he felt that Chrysippus had overlooked it.   Perhaps this usefulness in scientific reasoning is why modern logicians have chosen alternation as a fundamental logical constant rather than the exclusive disjunction, which Chrysippus made fundamental.

Sections 4, 5, 6

Just as the third indemonstrable, resting on incomplete conflict may have only an affirmative minor premiss, since the members of the major may be false together, so the paradisjunctive may have only a negative minor premiss.   Nevertheless, since it may have more than two members, it has two types of premiss, depending on whether some of the members, short of all but one, are denied, or all but one.

The syllogisms possible with the paradisjunctive should be compared with the complex case of the disjunctive with more than one member, which, as given in Chapter V, had complete conflict among all the members but incomplete among any less number of them.   There, there was one affirmative premiss, asserting the truth of one member and one negative premiss, denying all but one member.   The first premiss is similar to the affirmative premiss with a two-membered disjunctive; the second premiss is like the premiss of the paradisjunctive, denying all but one member.   With a two-membered paradisjunctive there would be only one premiss, the denial of one member, just as in the case of incomplete conflict there is only an affirmative premiss, asserting one member.

There is textual corruption in section 6: the first clause reads: *kai trión men mallona meinon to tetarton*.   Without conjecturing a reading, I have translated what the original must have meant.   It may be guessed that *ameinon* conceals a form of *menô*.

Sections 7, 8

It may be that Galen is refuting the opinion of someone who did maintain that the conditional form given was identical in force to the paradisjunctive.   In any case, his problem shows the difficulty that his rejection of formalism leads to.   Since he has no formal distinction between the disjunctive and the paradisjunctive, there can be no formal isolation of the type of conditional treated here from one with a disjunctive consequent.   If there were any use in a conditional of this sort, Galen's system prevents its being used.

Galen seems to present the syllogisms of the paradisjunctive as indemonstrables.   His originality seems apparent here; that it exists is confirmed by his use of an example from his own special field.   However, his denial in Chapter XIV, 3, that there are more than five indemonstrables appears a piece of carelessness, unless he meant the denial historically, that the Stoics recognized no more than the five.   Perhaps he did not mean them to be indemonstrable but did not feel it necessary to show how they could be demonstrated.

Section 9

The translation of the last clause of this section departs from Kalbfleisch's text.   "Exist" translates *huparchein*, Kalbfleisch's correction of the MS. *huparchontos*, which is clearly wrong.   Kalbfleisch's infinitive must depend on an implied assertion contained in the mention of a proslepsis.   It is assumed in the translation that the affirmative of *hyparchein* is to be supplied with the first member of the clause, not the negative.   In this case, Galen is stating the two forms of proslepsis with the disjunctive that make up the fourth and fifth indemonstrable, extending the pattern to disjunctives having more than two members. Otherwise, there seems to be no real distinction between the syllogisms with paradisjunctive majors and those with disjunctives.

It may be indicative of an attempt to devise a formal distinction between disjunctive and paradisjunctive that Galen has given as an example of a paradisjunctive one in which the verbs of the member clauses are participles, while, when the same example is stated as a disjunctive, the verbs are in the indicative mood.   Apparently, the participial form was felt to suggest that the actions could coexist, all or some, while the indicative statement emphasized their absolute disjunction.

Sections 10, 11

With the quotation from Plato's *Alcibiades I* (106d) Galen shows by example his distinction between the conditional with disjunctive or paradisjunctive consequent and the paradisjunctive. In the first case, he says, Plato, using the second indemonstrable, by denying both members of the disjunctive, denies the consequent of the conditional. Hence he infers the falsity of the antecedent, that Alcibiades knows justice. In the second case the denial of one member of the disjunctive implies the truth of the other.

CHAPTER XVI

Sections 1 through 5

These sections introduce the topic of relational syllogisms and give examples of them.

The name is given literally as syllogisms constructed "in accordance with the category of relation (*prosti*)."

The "Skeptics," according to Prantl (I, 606), may well be physicians of the Skeptical school of medicine. Perhaps, however, the term means any investigators who proceed in quasi-mathematical ways. Given Plato's habit of representing Socrates as using analogies and often uttering the work *skepteon* or its cognates, Galen may have had Plato or Platonists in mind, perhaps with some reference to the skepticism of the New Academy. He himself has used *skepsin poieisthai* in Chapter XIII, 8, in the sense of to investigate a question in physical science. He does not refer to skeptics elsewhere in the *Institutio*.

The statement that the disciples of Aristotle try to force relational syllogisms into the number of the categoricals has caused comment, since he sets out in section 6 to "reduce" them to categorical form. (See the commentary on that section.) Alexander of Aphrodisias (*in Anal. Pr.*, Wallies, 344ff) does the very thing Galen accuses the Peripatetics of; he maintains that arguments of this sort are defective categorical syllogisms. It is possible that Galen is here attacking Alexander. According to the Arabian commentators there was enmity between the two men, and Alexander had a low opinion of Galen's logical abilities (references in Mueller, *Beweis*, p. 22). Galen repeats his charge of "forcing" in section 9.

The reference to mathematicians calls to mind Galen's autobiographical remark (*De Libris Propriis*, Ch. XI, Kuehn, XIX) to the effect that he had found the logical teaching of all the schools of philosophy unsatisfactory in giving an account of demonstration and that he would have fallen into the school of the Pyrrhonians had he not seen that in geometry a sound method of proof existed, which was in fact praised by all schools. It is noteworthy that in the first chapter of the *Institutio* he gives a mathematical example of the method of demonstration.

The examples given in the first four sections of this chapter are all mathematical, or rather, arithmetical examples. The care with which Galen states them reveals the fact that he considers them as likely to be unfamiliar to the general reader and that he is aware that he is dealing with a new subject matter. But this very fact is somewhat puzzling. As will be made clear later, there is evidence that these syllogisms, treated in somewhat the same order as here, had been treated by previous writers. The reference to Posidonius at the end of Chapter XVIII points to his having dealt with them, and probably rather fully. At least the reference suggests a fairly systematic treatment, implying a classification scheme underlying his treatment. Yet the rare use of the first person in the first sentence of this chapter seems to imply some kind of a claim to originality of treatment on Galen's part. Actually, all that is attributed to Posidonius at the close of the discussion is the characterization "conclusive by force of axiom"; the naming of the genus as relational is asserted on Galen's authority alone. Therefore, it seems probable that he claims for himself the recognition that the syllogisms under discussion deal with things in relation and that the part played by axioms was what he learned from Posidonius. Further evidence in support of this view may be found in the fact that Alexander treats the same type of argument under the title, borrowed from the Stoics, of *amethodoi perainontes*. Galen mentions this title in the chapter following the discussion of relational syllogisms, separating them and, in fact, considering arguments that conclude unmethodically as hardly worthy of notice. It is most probable, then, that he felt that he had given an account of the method of these arguments and was entitled to the credit of recognizing that they had a method. The nerve of Galen's position seems to be that he shows, or thinks he has shown, that the method is general for all terms of relation and is not confined to mathematical subjects.

In section 5 Galen introduces the term which he finally attributes to Posidonius, saying that all the arguments have in common the fact that they derive the cause of their structure (*systasis*) from certain axioms. At this point the reader still must refer the statement to the arithmetical examples. The generalization of the method comes later.

The contradiction between section 1 and section 5, that in section 1 Galen says that the Peripatetics try to force the relational syllogisms into the number of the categoricals, while in section 5 he himself promises to reduce them to the categorical form, is more apparent than real. Aristotle himself reduced syllogisms of the second and third figures to those of the first, without destroying the distinction of the figures. Galen, thus, may be able to show how his syllogisms can be "reduced" to categorical form, but still not mean that relational syllogisms are a defective form of categoricals.

Sections 6 through 9

Galen's "reduction" may be compared with Alexander's discussion of the same example (*in Anal. Pr.*, Wallies, 344):

> Wherefore it is not the case, if taking A equal to B and B equal to C it follows necessarily that A is equal to C, that this is already a syllogism.   It will be syllogistically concluded, if, taking an additional premiss, a universal, which says, "Things equal to the same thing are also equal to each other," we compress the two taken premisses into one premiss, which is equivalent to the two; this is: "A and C are equal to the same thing (i.e., B)"; for thus it is concluded in the manner of a syllogism that A and C are equal to each other.

It is possible to reduce the difference between Galen and Alexander to the meaning of the word syllogism.   Alexander understands by it categorical syllogism, while Galen means any conclusive argument, whether in the form of an Aristotelian syllogism or not.   But taken in conjunction with Alexander's attempt to show that the Chrysippean indemonstrable syllogisms really depend on a categorical syllogism for their validity, it is hard to escape the conclusion that Alexander considers the categorical syllogism the one true form of logically conclusive reasoning.

Galen's conception of the role played by an axiom in a demonstrative syllogism is different.   Though he nowhere says so explicitly, it is apparent from his handling of his examples that he thinks of the particular syllogism as consisting of a substitution of definite terms of the subject under discussion for the general term "things" which occurs in the axiom. Thus, Galen's point of view is essentially that of the modern symbolic logician, who calls the general terms of the axioms or logical laws "variables," and the definite terms of the application of the law "constants."   From this point of view, Galen would be justified in turning on the Peripatetics and saying, your categorical syllogisms consist in a process of substituting in an axiom, for instance the syllogism *Barbara*, certain terms for particular things in place of the symbols A, B, and C.

Galen's discussion so far confuses the two principles he has enunciated: one, that relations occur in a special class of syllogisms, and two, that these syllogisms depend for their structure on an "axiom."   Sections 6, 7, and 8 are apparently clear.   The examples given are of demonstrations involving the relative term "equal to" and he can show easily enough that such arguments derive their force from one or another of the Euclidian Common Notions having to do with equality.   In section 9, however, his example is of the relations double and quadruple.   He repeats his example of section 1, in more abstract terms, but does not identify the axiom he supposes the argument to depend on.   It seems as if here he treats the abstract statement as axiomatic in relation to the concrete case of the comparison of what Dion, Theon, and Philon possess. But in Chapter XVIII, section 6, he shows that all statements of proportion which name definite numerical ratios depend on a universal statement of proportion, in effect Euclid's definition of numerical proportion. The example in section 9, however, still does not fall under this definition but under the definition of continuous proportion. It would seem that Galen has not thought through the problem completely. It could not, in fact, be treated adequately until the symbols of complete generality of numbers, the algebraic letter-numbers, were available for use.

Galen or his source has discovered that there are relations that are transitive, or symmetrical, or reciprocal and that inferences may be made from these properties. He also observes that the mathematicians make use of these properties of the relations "equal" and "more or less than" and define the operations with these relations in the Common Notions or Axioms. Next he generalizes from these numerical relations to others exhibiting one or more of the properties. Then he generalizes the description of relational syllogisms and gives to them the common property of depending on an axiom. Afterward, he goes on to the discovery that there are other kinds of syllogisms that depend on an axiom for their validity, with the result that as his discussion continues it becomes somewhat confusing to the reader. But our confusion need not obscure for us his contribution to the theory of logic.

One qualification must be kept in mind. It is not likely that the material in this and the following two chapters are entirely original with Galen. As already remarked, discussion of arguments of this kind is reflected in other writers—Cicero, Apuleius, Sextus, for instance. If this discussion, in fact, dates back to the school of Posidonius, there was, in all probability, some systematic treatment of relational syllogisms and of axiomatics before Galen.

Section 10

In this section Galen asserts the extension of the form he has been analyzing in arithmetical proofs to other arguments involving relative terms; specifically, he asserts that the structure of such syllogisms will depend on the "conjoining" of an axiom. Therefore, it is puzzling that in the example he gives there is no sign of an axiom, just an argument depending on the reciprocal relation of the terms father and son. It is true that in section 11, where he states the argument in categorical form, he states a "certain general axiom," namely: "The man whom someone has as father, of him he is the son." This amounts to an assertion of the reciprocal relation implied by the terms "father" and "son." But

Galen expressly says that this form of the argument is forced. We are therefore left in the dark as to how Galen believes the axiom should be stated for the argument as given in this section.

Referring back to the earlier sections, however, it will be recalled that Galen gives no explicit statement of the axiom that validates the arguments until he states them in categorical form. Perhaps he means that an argument stated in the form in which, in each case, he first gives it, so obviously reveals in its statement the self-evident truth which makes it cogent that it is unnecessary to give it verbal expression. Thus, the Peripatetic insistence on making the axiom one of the premisses of the syllogism would seem to him pedantic and forced.

The discussion so far has maintained that an axiom is the cause of the structure (i.e., cogency) of all arguments making inferences from terms signifying relations. There is not yet any hint that axioms are required in other forms of arguments.

Section 11

Galen has said, in section 1 of this chapter, that the relational syllogisms are a third kind of syllogism. Obviously, he means a third kind in addition to the categorical and the hypothetical. It is odd, then, that in this section he makes the three kinds convertible into each other. He seems to have been misled by the fact that in section 10 he sets out the argument in a conditional sentence. His missing axiom, really a definition of the father-son relationship as a reciprocal relation, is taken for granted. The argument is an immediate inference, granting the definition. Now he sees the need for a minor premiss asserting it as a fact that Socrates is the son of Sophroniscus. His previous statement has merely replaced the general terms of the definition with the names of particular persons. So the argument falls naturally into the hypothetical form of the first indemonstrable. The same minor premiss, taken in conjunction with the axiom itself of the father-son relationship, creates, in a more forced way, a categorical syllogism. Yet it is not really a categorical syllogism; neither of the terms of the minor premiss occur in the major. The major premiss Galen gives is, in fact, Galen's "axiom." The correct major premiss is: "He who has Socrates as father, is the son of Socrates," substituting the name Socrates for the indefinite pronouns of the "axiom." The best explanation, or excuse, for Galen's confusing presentation is that Galen, as he has already said, does not conceive of logic as attending to the verbal form of the argument, but to the logical relations. He thus expects his reader to follow him in recognizing the logical relations implicit in the wording he gives, but at the cost of making the reader uncertain, when he reaches this point in the discussion, as to just what the difference is between the three classes of syllogisms.

Sections 12, 13

The point of these sections seems to be that the dependence of relational arguments for their cogency on general axioms extends beyond numbers and things in the category of relation (*prosti*). This is indicated by the use of the word *schesis*, which Euclid uses as a generic term in his definition of ratio (V, 3). In discussing syllogisms of arithmetic, Galen gives examples mainly of arguments involving equality, though in the argument about the double of the double he touched on one example of a transitive relation of greater and less. His first move out of the realm of number was to terms (father-son) expressing relationship in their meaning. Now he generalizes to relations between non-relative and non-arithmetical terms. In effect, he seems to be saying that anything in the world that is capable of having as predicate an adjective in the comparative degree, whether expressed by grammatical inflection or by the use of the word more,* may enter, with its predicate, into a relational syllogism, and that this syllogism will derive its conclusive force from a general axiom. Unfortunately, he chooses at this point to refer the reader for examples to another of his writings, the commentaries on the word *mallon*. In the examples of arguments using comparative adjectives, he has, however, given an indication of how he conceives of his general axiom. "The virtue of the better is worthier of choice" (than the virtue of the less good) serves as a major premiss in a categorical syllogism. Apparently he believes that he is laying bare the logical structure of the kind of argument exemplified in Aristotle's: "Soul is better than body, health is a good, therefore virtue is a good." Yet Galen's major premiss is hardly a self-evident axiom, since it depends on a more general axiom, such as "Properties of better things are better than properties of their inferiors." This formulation, perhaps, equivocates on the word better; in the first case meaning "more honorable" or better on some scale of values of substance, while in the second case meaning more worthy of choice. The equivocation is, however, mine rather than Galen's. The difficulty is that terms like better and worthier of choice seem to restrict the propositions in which they occur to a scope somewhat less than is to be expected of a general axiom. It seems probable, nevertheless, that Galen considered the premiss, in the form in which he gives it, to be a self-evident truth. (Aristotle, *Topics*, 114 b 38, on the topic "more or less.")

Another question with regard to his examples in these sections is

---

* Galen refers to comparative adjectives as expressing meaning *kata dynamin* of the word "more," without the word. This phrase is the same as that used at the end of Chapter XVIII in the attribution to Posidonius of the phrase "*kata dynamin*" of an axiom. The phrase also occurs in Chapter XV, 10, where it means something like "implicitly."

whether he considered that the argument in the form he gives it is a categorical syllogism, or that it belongs to his distinct class of relational syllogisms.   If he has, as I suppose, intended his last cases to involve terms that do not fall under the category *prosti*, then the arguments could not, in view of his name for the class, belong to the class.   Yet he obviously intends that they do.   He is here paying for his unwillingness to accept the verbal or symbolic form of the argument as characteristic of the class of syllogism.   Perhaps he means that a true categorical syllogism must have all its terms non-relative.   Yet this interpretation is made difficult by the fact that in Chapter XVIII, 6, he gives an example of an argument in categorical form in the category *prosti*.   This latter example, however, is rather sketchily alluded to and perhaps he would not maintain that it is to be taken with complete seriousness.

Galen's exposition of the relational syllogisms is made a little cumbersome by the fact that the assignment of terms to the category *prosti*, as made by Aristotle and apparently concurred in by ancient thinkers, with the possible exception of the Stoics, is carried out under the conception of the relation inhering in a substance, e.g., a father is related to a son by something more than juxtaposition.   The use of comparative adjectives, however, pointed to many sentences in which things unrelated otherwise were brought into relation.   Therefore, Galen felt he had to exemplify separately arguments constructed with such terms.

Chapter XVI as a whole presents the first stage of an exposition of a separate class of syllogisms, which Galen names relational.   His insistence that they draw the cogency of their demonstrative force from an axiom is really an attempt at an analysis of the nature of relation.   As has been seen, Galen is not entirely clear about this nature, but he does recognize that what makes relational arguments cogent is derived from their transitivity, their symmetry, their reciprocity, or a combination of these properties.   He goes part of the way toward freeing the concept of relation from the restrictions imposed by the doctrine of Aristotle's *Categories*, yet does not have at hand or develop a terminology that is capable of making the distinctions he is aware of clear and capable of further development.   His treatment of the subject is also noteworthy because it brings together the form of reasoning in mathematics with forms used in other subject matters; this is a different enterprise from the use that Aristotle makes of mathematical examples in the *Posterior Analytics*.   There Aristotle analyzes mathematical arguments as if they fell under the system of the categorical syllogism and as if there was no essential difference in the way mathematicians reason and the general method of reasoning which he studies in the *Analytics*.   From the point of view of later logic, Galen's results may not be impressive, but, whether original with him or not, they are a serious attempt to find and generalize the principles of mathematical reasoning.

CHAPTER XVII
Sections 1 through 4

Galen begins a new chapter with a further generalization about the part played by axioms in the conclusiveness of syllogisms. His opening sentence certainly extends the role of the axiom to "nearly all syllogisms." An axiom as root of cogency, therefore, is no longer the distinguishing mark of the relational syllogism but is a property of (nearly) all syllogisms. How seriously to take the qualifier is a question. It seems best to take it as a mark of caution and to assume that Galen means all syllogisms with which he is acquainted, not that he is aware of exceptions to the rule.

By rights, then, the statement must apply to the categorical and hypothetical syllogisms. Unfortunately, Galen does not expressly say this, and there are no examples given in this chapter of plain categorical or hypothetical syllogisms illustrating the rule. The chapter, however, is one of the most corrupt textually in the book, so that the possibility exists that there were such illustrations. If so, there is no trace of them in the text we have. More probably, Galen would say that the indemonstrable syllogisms of the first figure among the categoricals and the five indemonstrables of Chrysippus are the axioms for arguments in these forms. The examples he does give are of more complicated reasonings.

His remark that he had not understood this property of all syllogisms until after he had written *De Demonstratione* and *De Numero Syllogismorum* is one indication supporting the authenticity of the book. It is a characteristic of Galen to refer frequently to his other works and to offer supplements and corrections to their content. It is also evidence that the work represents thinking on Galen's part and is not a mere compilation from other sources. For whether or not he worked out this axiom theory for himself, he certainly allows his mind to play over its implications in a way that is not consistent with simple reproduction of another's thought.

The first example Galen adduces to illustrate his remark shows that he had read some discussions of these arguments, probably in Stoic sources. For the type of argument, the truth-teller, is discussed by Alexander, in slightly different form, in two places of his commentary on the *Prior Analytics*. The briefer treatment (Wallies, p. 21) reads as follows:

And in general such is the form of the arguments which the younger (philosophers) call "unmethodically concluding," such as is the argument:
It is day; but also you say that it is day; therefore you speak the truth.
For this is not a syllogism; but it will be one with the addition of the universal premiss, "He who says that what is, is, speaks the truth."

In his longer discussion (Wallies, pp. 344ff) Alexander gives the same example with more detail.   He uses the stock name Dion and he implies that the addition of the universal premiss converts the argument to a categorical syllogism.   Alexander's usage elsewhere shows that by the younger philosophers he means either the Stoics in general or the more recent Stoics.   Both in Galen and in Alexander the discussion indicates that they were drawing from writers who were elaborating and systematizing logical doctrine.   Alexander's statements prove that Galen could not, however, have acquired his theory of a universal axiom from these writers, since the point of his criticism is that they believed the argument was conclusive even though it stated no universal premiss.   On the other hand, Galen seems to differ from Alexander in making the universal an axiom rather than any universal proposition.   Alexander, in effect, is requiring that an argument, to be a syllogism, must contain an explicit statement of the propositions that enter into it, while Galen probably means that the argument is cogent even without the explicit statement of the relevant universal axiom, provided the given premisses are such as to reveal clearly their dependence on the axiom.   If this seems to be attributing a confused state of mind to Galen, one should refer to his criticism of Chrysippus in Chapter IV, 6, the point of which is that Chrysippus and his followers attend to the verbal expression (*lexis*) rather than to the matters (*tois pragmasin*).   Furthermore, there are examples in other works of Galen (e.g., Kuehn, IV, 609f) in which he says he will give the argument for his statement (on some medical or scientific point) in the form of a categorical syllogism.   In some such cases it is hard to see that what he says immediately afterward is verbally in the form of a categorical syllogism, though he gives the reader the material from which one may be constructed.   It looks, indeed, as if Galen's view is that a syllogism is a mental act, the verbal form of which is relatively unimportant.   If this is so, then he must conceive of syllogisms cogent "by force of an axiom" as containing the axiom, whether or not it is expressed in words.   In other words, on this view, Galen would make no distinction between an enthymeme, in the modern sense, and a complete syllogism.   As we have seen (in ch. XVI, 12), *kata dynamin*, "by force of" is used when something is meant but not stated.

Aside from the question of form, there is a difference between Galen and Alexander in the presentation of the "truth-teller."   From the fact that Dion says that it is day, one may either add that it is day and conclude that Dion speaks the truth; or one may take it as given that Dion always speaks the truth and conclude that it is day.   Galen gives only the second argument, while Alexander, in the longer passage, gives both forms but shows more interest in the first.   By discussing the second argument, Galen involves himself in certain complexities.   With the premiss "Dion always speaks the truth," Galen introduces, although not altogether consciously, the use of arguments from authority.   This is clear when he says at the end of the chapter that "Dion always speaks the truth" is taken in place of the universal axiom.   Such a premiss would only be possible in the status of a universal axiom if there were a kind of universal consensus about someone that this was the case.   One thinks of Galen's belief in the near infallibility of Plato and Hippocrates.   On the other hand, the first form of the argument will work with anyone.   All that is needed is that his statement may be verified by reference to the facts.   A congenital liar may, on occasion, make a true statement.   The fact that Galen is interested in the second form is consistent with his whole view of logic as the practical art of demonstration.   He constantly used the authority of his two heroes in making his own demonstrations.

The complexity in Galen's discussion comes about from the fact that, (1) as has just been said, one facet of it consists of the assumption of the possibility to substitute for a universal axiom a proposition derived from the axiom by substituting a proper name for the indefinite pronoun of the axiom; (2) that this analysis immediately shows that two logical operations take place; and (3) that there is still a further inference from "it is true that . . ." to "it is."   Galen is aware, also, of this second duplication, since he restates the argument in section 8 to bring out that very point.   The operation of substituting a proper name in the axiom is stated in section 9.

In these sections and in the rest of this chapter, it is safe to say that Galen is reporting and perhaps elaborating, a discussion of logic that goes beyond the traditional treatment of categorical and hypothetical syllogisms.   The discussion has moved logicians toward the tenets of modern logicians, especially with regard to substitution and to the use of a metalanguage.   The truth-teller argument depends on the fact that true and false are predicates of a proposition taken as a subject.   Galen obscures this fact by saying in section 4 that "it is true that it is day" is equivalent to "it is day" in the same way that the statement that a thing exists is equivalent to the statement that it is, and the latter is equivalent to the statement that there is something existent and that it is.   The third equivalence, if it means anything, is merely a more precise way of saying that something is, while the second asserts that "exists" and "is" are synonyms and, by implication, that one synonym may be substituted for another in a sentence without changing its meaning.   The first equivalence, however, in the modern view, is not an equivalence at all. One part of it asserts that a certain proposition is true, while the other part of it asserts the proposition itself.   The first is a statement about a proposition, the second is a statement about something in the world outside of thought.   Thus the two are propositions in different universes of discourse and cannot be strictly equivalent.   Nevertheless, the recognition that there is a logical relation between the two propositions is an important advance in the history of logic.

Note that the words of the section, "says the same as he who says, 'It is day'," are Kalbfleisch's conjecture to fill in a lacuna in the text. Comparison with section 8, however, makes the conjecture practically certain.

Sections 5 through 9

Mention of these equivalent propositions leads Galen, as so often, into a digression on that subject. He is rather prone to such digressions when the subject under discussion is one on which he has already written a book. He has told us elsewhere that he has written a book with the title *On Equivalent Propositions*. The last sentence of section 5 is mutilated, so that we do not know what his example was and so cannot find out precisely what he has in mind in contrasting with equivalent sentences ones which do not "say the same thing but obviously have opposite meanings." Perhaps he is thinking of pairs of sentences, not on their face contradictory, but easily seen to be so when the meanings of their terms are examined. At any rate, the remark is an aside, which has little relevance to the subject under discussion except to lead into the discussion in the following sections of the importance of attention to meanings of terms.

In section 6, then, he submits the position with regard to the use of terms which he has already implied in earlier chapters of the book: words are to be used in their common Greek meaning. He is the foe of all pettifogging and overelaborate distinctions. His illustration by the definition of "truth" is interesting as it is the definition given by Plato and Aristotle. In general, Galen follows the terminology of Aristotle, so that his notion of what all Greeks commonly mean by a word seems to be based on the criterion of the usage of Aristotle and his school.

Section 7 summarizes the preceding section by following the rule that attention to the correct Greek meaning of the terms used is of prime importance in reasoning, while it is of equal importance to note whether the argument depends on an axiom—axiom understood as self-evident proposition. This return to the axiom theme is, unfortunately, of little help in understanding whether Galen means to suggest an alternative syllogistic structure to one depending on an axiom. When he allows the possibility of some other reason he is vague and does not say whether he knows of any other approach. Certainly, the section says that most reasoning depends on an axiom. The large number of discussions of reasoning with which he was familiar and the confusion introduced into these discussions by the rivalries of the different schools must have imposed caution on him as the writer of an elementary textbook.

In section 8 Galen returns to the analysis of the truth-teller argument. Here he dissects the arguments into the stages already suggested in section 3, but more explicitly and precisely.   First Galen places the definition of truth, then that Dion always speaks the truth, then that he asserts that there is divination, and then the conclusion, that divination exists.   Thus we see here explicitly the two logical operations that were noticed in the comment on section 3.   Dion is substituted in the definition of the truth-teller to lead to the conclusion that he makes a true assertion.   Then from the predication of truth to Dion's assertion, the right to assert it truly follows.   Section 9 makes explicit the fact that there is the substitution of the singular name Dion for the pronoun in the general definition of the truth-teller.   Thus, although Galen's account is lacking in systematic expression of the logical form in this argument, his example clearly reveals the structure of it.

CHAPTER XVIII

In this chapter Galen returns to relational syllogisms.   But here he reverses his manner of exposition from that of Chapter XVI.   There he began with mathematical arguments and went on to exhibit analogous forms of reasoning in non-mathematical subjects.   Here, however, he begins with an example from Plato's *Republic*, the analogy between the soul and the city, and then goes on to the mathematical form of proportion. In Plato, the analogy of city to soul allows the conclusion from the more easily determined ratio of justice in the city to the same ratio holding true in the soul.   The bulk of the chapter is made up of a rather lengthy explanation of mathematical proportion.   The general definition of proportion, that A is to B as C is to D allows the conclusion that if the ratio of A to B is of certain numbers, then that of C to D is of the same numbers.

There is no discussion of the extension of the concept of ratio and proportion to magnitude that is the nub of Euclid's fifth book.   This is unnecessary to Galen's exposition.   Galen is satisfied to show that the meaning of "likewise" can be reduced to a general form, expressible mathematically but applicable over a wider range of terms; and that then, on the basis of this general axiom, particular arguments may be constructed.   Here again, what he is really presenting is a method of substitution of definite terms for indefinite, of constants for variables, in modern terminology.

In the concluding section of the chapter, section 8, Galen is again confusing.   "All these syllogisms" may be just those of this chapter or they may include those of Chapter XVI as well.   They cannot include those of Chapter XVII, which are not relational.   Since he has apparently

said that all relational syllogisms, and possibly all syllogisms, are conclusive by force of an axiom, it is difficult to see how this latter qualification
can be a species of the genus relational syllogism.   It is possibly the case
that he has condensed his exposition here, and that the sources from
which he drew distinguished more clearly between syllogisms depending
on self-evident truths and those depending on definitions, which would
be self-evident in the sense that, when once constructed, they are
necessarily taken as governing the course of the argument.   In the
ancient view of definition, there need be nothing arbitrary, if the definition
is a so-called real definition.   Yet the self-evident axiom is different from
a definition.   The latter is a statement of the nature or essence of a
substance, while an axiom is a predication of something of a subject
which is self-evident to the reason and perfectly general in its application.

The quotation from Posidonius is tantalizing in its lack of relation to
anything else that has been said.   Whether Posidonius used the phrase
"by force of axiom" in reference to the kinds of arguments Galen has
been discussing or in a different context, and Galen has borrowed the
phrase for his own purpose, is unclear.   The "them" seems to refer to
the arguments discussed, but it is not impossible that Posidonius was
talking exclusively about mathematical arguments.   It is further unclear
whether Posidonius is to be held responsible for the arguments being
called relational as well as "conclusive by force of axiom."   Certainly,
the latter words are all that are directly attributed to Posidonius, but the
inference is open that he applied the term to relational syllogisms.   It
seems more likely, on the basis of Galen's whole discussion, that he does
not draw the concept of relational syllogisms from Posidonius.   If this
is true, it becomes more likely that Galen's claim that he invented the
term is to be extended to his recognition of the class of such syllogisms,
although undoubtedly particular forms of them were known and discussed
by earlier logicians.   As implied earlier, the point of Posidonius's phrase
may be a classification of certain arguments, somehow deriving conclusiveness from an axiom which nevertheless is not expressed in the
argument.

CHAPTER XIX

In this final chapter Galen deals briefly with certain forms of argument
which had been discussed by logicians since Aristotle, but which he
considers superfluous.   In the first four sections he treats a form called
"by assumption."

The term he uses for "assumption" is *proslêpsis*.   This word occurs in
one passage only of the *Prior Analytics* (58 b 9) where Ross brackets the
clause in which it occurs, on the ground that the word is Theophrastean.

Alexander discusses the term and distinguishes it from *metalêpsis* (Wallies, 263f). The latter he says is used by Aristotle and the Peripatetics for the minor premiss of a hypothetical syllogism, called by the Stoics, the *neoteroi* (Alexander uses both terms here synonymously) *proslêpsis*. Alexander understands the distinction to be that a *metalêpsis* repeats a clause contained in the hypothetical major premiss, only stating it as an assertion instead of as a hypothesis. The Aristotelian usage of *proslêpsis*, Alexander continues, denotes a premiss that is not contained actually (*energei*) in the major. He then goes on: "As it is in the syllogisms that come about *kata proslêpsis*: for in the syllogisms of what B is predicated, of this A, but of C, B, the premiss of C, B is assumed 'from without' (*exôthen*): for that premiss is not contained actually in the premiss 'of what B, of that A'."

Galen rightly points out in section 5 that the formulation given here is merely an abbreviation of the ordinary form of categorical syllogism and since he has already pointed this out in *De Demonstratione*, he need spend no more time on it here. Note the implied conditional form of universal affirmative.

Alexander, however, seems merely to be discussing the terms *metalêpsis* and *proslêpsis*. It seems that he considers them terms for the minor premisses, respectively, of hypothetical and categorical syllogisms. No doubt other Peripatetics had offered this formulation as a distinct form of syllogism and Galen felt it necessary to reject it.

Alexander, however, does not consistently hold to this distinction between *proslêpsis* and *metalêpsis*. For in commenting on *Prior Analytics* (50 a 16, Wallies, 386ff), a passage in which Aristotle discusses arguments *ex hypotheseôs*, he seems to refer to the hypothesis as either a *proslêpsis* or a *metalêpsis*. Alexander (388, 17) quotes Theophrastus, as apparently using the term *proslêpsis* in this sense. Galen, at any rate, does not discuss this form of argument. Plainly he used the Stoic term but in a wider sense than the Stoics used it. It is possible that Galen confused here the different kinds of argument by *proslêpsis* and thought that the Peripatetic commentators were offering the formulation he gives as a different kind of syllogism, when, in fact, they considered only the *ex hypotheseôs* as standing in need of special explanation. It is, finally, interesting that here again Galen's discussion touches on something that Alexander had dealt with. It would be worthwhile to discover whether Galen knew the work of Alexander, or whether he drew from one of Alexander's predecessors. The latter is the more probable supposition.

In his concluding section he briefly scorns many of the syllogistic forms of his *bête noir*, Chrysippus, especially the "unmethodical" arguments, making the commonsense remark that they are superfluous. It is a pity that the works in which he rejects these syllogisms is lost. It might throw great light on the formalism of Stoic logic.

Appendix
Who are the neoteroi?

In the third chapter of the *Institutio* Galen gives two pairs of names for the two main hypothetical propositions, the conditional and the disjunctive. The terms "hypothetical by connection" and "separative" or "hypothetical by separation" are said to be those of the *palaioi*, while "conjunctive" (*sunêmmenon*) and "disjunctive" (*diezeugmenon*) are used for the same propositions by the *neoteroi*. The substantive used or understood with these adjectives is *philosophoi*.

It is the usual interpretation that the *palaioi* are the Peripatetics and the *neoteroi* the Stoics. This seems to be substantially the case, but the question is not simple. Part of the argument for the case is that terms and doctrines associated in reports with these names are respectively Peripatetic and Stoic. But on the other hand, some of the evidence offered that a particular term or doctrine is Stoic is that it is reported to be held by the *neoteroi*. Thus there is an element of circularity that must be avoided.

A second question about *neoteroi* is whether it means Stoics simply or later members of the Stoic sect. Or whether the pair of names is purely chronological and no implication of a doctrine of a particular philosophical school is intended.

This note will offer an examination of the usage of writers, especially Alexander, in order to determine as far as possible who is meant when these names are used.

The general sense of *neoteroi* in a non-philosophical context is seen in Cicero's use of it to label the younger poets of his day, a use which, as is well known, has contemptuous overtones. Probably the meaning of *neoterizein* "to revolutionize" contributed something to its connotation. The modern use of "modern," with shades of approbation or disapproval depending on the point of view of the speaker, has something in common with this usage.

In philosophical contexts we find Plutarch (adv. Col. 15) calling *neoteroi* the holders of certain doctrines, which some passages in Sextus Empiricus (Pyrrh., II, 107; *Adv. Math.*, VIII, 13) show to be Epicurean. In *de Placitis Hippocratis et Platonis*, Galen several times cites against the opinions of Chrysippus the opinions of *hoi palaioi*, who, the context shows, include Zeno. (One such passage is found on p. 348 of Mueller's edition.) Sextus (*Adv. Math.*, 253) contrasts the views of *hoi archaioteroi* of the Stoics with those of *hoi neoteroi*, with regard to the "criterion." Thus in these passages and others like them the names seem to be used somewhat flexibly and in reference to chronological sequence rather than to philosophical schools.

In Alexander's commentaries on the *Prior Analytics* and the *Topics*, we find most of the evidence that would connect the term *neoteroi* more closely with the Stoics.

The most important passage, in that it has to do with fundamental logical doctrine, occurs at *in Prior Analytics* (Wallies, 262, 38). Commenting on Aristotle's discussion of arguments from a "hypothesis" (*Anal. Pr.*, 41 a, 37) Alexander says:

> (such arguments) would be those the *neoteroi* maintain are the only syllogisms: these are those that are composed of a "tropic," as they call it, and an additional premiss (*proslêpsis*), the tropic being either a conditional, a disjunctive, or a conjunction, the old (archaioi) writers call these "mixed" of an hypothetical premiss and a declarative, i.e., a categorical.

The syllogisms described in this passage are clearly the five indemonstrables of Chrysippus. Moreover, Galen attests the term "tropic" for Chrysippus in the first section of Chapter VII of the *Institutio*. He also attests *proslêpsis* as the regular term for the minor premiss of the hypothetical syllogism, as Alexander does, too, in other passages. Galen does not give the older term "mixed" for these syllogisms, but Albinus, Galen's teacher, does in Chapter VI of his introduction to Platonic philosophy. Certainly, then, the *neoteroi* are here associated with the doctrine and terms of Chrysippus. It should be noted, however, that the assertion attributed to the *neoteroi* is that the hypotheticals are the only syllogisms. This assertion is unlikely to be Chrysippus's. The long list of his logical works given by Diogenes Laertius suggests that Chrysippus recognized many kinds of syllogisms. Alexander's *neoteroi* here could be later writers on logic, perhaps not even Stoics, who adopted the five indemonstrables as the only syllogisms. Perhaps this notice refers to the same discussion that is reflected in Galen's statement that Boethos called them primary.

Connected with the five indemonstrables, as we read in several writers, among them Galen, *Hippocrates and Plato*, were four "themata." These were logical procedures by which a complex argument could be analyzed into one or more of the indemonstrables.   Alexander mentions (*in Anal. Pr.*, Wallies, 284, 13) that *hoi apo tês Stoas* developed the second, third, and fourth themata from Aristotle's procedures for reducing syllogisms to the first figure.   Then at 278, 6 and 164, 27, he attributes a thema to the *neoteroi*.   Again, the *neoteroi* deal with Stoic material, but it is noteworthy that while the invention of the themata is ascribed to the Stoics, the reference to the *neoteroi* merely says that they call a certain device the second or the third thema.   Here again these people may be later writers discussing Stoic material.

A point of terminology that Alexander mentions several times is the use of *metalêpsis* or *proslêpsis* as a name for the minor premiss.   The former is the Peripatetic term, he tells us, the latter the term of the *neoteroi* (*in Anal. Pr.*, 19, 3; Wallies, 262, 9; 263, 26) or of *hoi apo tês Stoas* (19, 21).   But Alexander himself occasionally uses *proslêpsis* for what he says is properly *metalêpsis*, so that the former term seems to have gradually become the standard term, irrespective of the schools.

Alexander remarks (Wallies, 390, 16) that for Aristotle hypothetical *logoi* are not syllogistic, but perantic, i.e., conclusive, while the *neoteroi* hold the opposite view.   Alexander (283, 13) says the *neoteroi* give the name *epiballontes kai epiballomenoi* to chains of reasonings that are kinds of sorites and develop them further than is practically useful.   This discussion ends in the passage already quoted ascribing to the Stoics the invention of the themata.   This name is rather unusual and not connected in the sources with Chrysippus.   It looks once more as if Alexander's *neoteroi* are later writers who are interested in developing a standard terminology for logical forms and procedures.

Another focus on the reference of the term is provided by two passages, one in the commentary on *Anal. Pr.*, the other in that on the *Topics*. The former (*in Anal. Pr.*, Wallies, 17, 11) speaks of syllogisms called "single-premissed" by the *neoteroi*.   The same term for the same kind of argument is attributed to *hoi peri Antipatrou* (*in Top.*, 8, 16).   Since Sextus reports (*Adv. Math.*, VIII, 443) that Chrysippus rejected these single-premissed syllogisms, but that Antipater admitted them, this set of passages gives evidence that *neoteroi* could be used for the later members of the Stoic school and at least sometimes does not include Chrysippus.

The remaining attributions of opinions to *neoteroi* include references to various special forms of argument, the "diphoric" ("if p, then p"), the "undifferentiate" (affirming the antecedent and concluding the same), the "unmethodic" (which seems to have been a catch-all phrase for arguments that were valid but did not fall within the usual syllogistic rules).   Galen mentions such a rubric in his last chapter, possibly referring it to Chrysippus.   However, Galen treats under relational arguments some which Alexander gives as examples of the neoteric "unmethodic."   In one passage Alexander also attributes unmethodic arguments to the Stoics.   Lastly, among the arguments discussed by the *neoteroi*, Alexander mentions the hyposyllogistic.   These turn out to be alternative forms of a regular syllogism, with a premiss expressed in an equivalent but less usual form, e.g., "Not every . . ." in place of "Some . . . not" for the particular negative.

Lastly, Alexander accuses (*in Anal. Pr.*, 373, 28) the *neoteroi* of attending to verbal expression rather than meaning and in several places says that they work out useless syllogisms.   Galen has made this same charge specifically against Chrysippus.

The conclusion to be drawn from this review of the uses of *neoteroi* is that in a logical context it refers to writers who dealt largely with a tradition stemming from Chrysippus.   The writers may be and probably were generally Stoics, but they need not have been.   The term connotes teachers of logical doctrine rather than originators, persons who have arranged under convenient labels the divisions of the subject matter of the science, and who have perhaps investigated the variations in linguistic form that make the use of ordinary language so troubling to the logician. The term was probably flexible enough so that at times it could include Chrysippus or at least his doctrines, while at other times it definitely represented a later stage in the history of logic.   In Alexander, at least, it has a derogatory sense, since he is concerned with demonstrating Aristotle's superiority to these later innovators.   In Galen's use the term is neutral, in conformity with his principle of indifference to terminological variation.

Bibliography

(Works consulted in preparing this commentary)

Texts of Galen's works

KALBFLEISCH, C. *Galeni Institutio Logica.* Leipzig, 1896.

KUEHN, C. *Claudii Galeni Opera Omnia.* 20 vols. Leipzig, 1821–1833.

MARQUARDT, VON MEULLER, HELMREICH. *Scripta Minora,* 3 vols. Leipzig, 1893.

VON MUELLER, I. *De Placitis Hippocratis et Platonis.* Leipzig, 1874.

BROCK, A. J. *On the Natural Faculties.* (Loeb Classical Library). Cambridge and London, 1947.

Translations (German)

MAU, J. *Galen, Einfuehrung in die Logik* (translation with commentary). Berlin, 1960.

ORTH, E. *Einfuehrung in die Logik.* Rome, 1938.

Works on Galen

KALBFLEISCH, KARL. *Ueber Galens Einleitung in die Logik.* Leipzig, 1897.

VON MUELLER, I. *Ueber Galens Werk vom Wissenschaftlichen Beweis.* Munich, 1895.

STAKELUM, J. W. *Galen and the Logic of Propositions.* Rome, 1940.

Other Ancient Authors

ALEXANDER, APHRODISIENSIS. *Commentary on Aristotle's Prior Analytics, Book I,* ed. M. WALLIES. Berlin, 1883.

——. *Commentary on Aristotle's Topics,* ed. M. WALLIES. Berlin, 1891.

APULEIUS. *De Dogmatibus Platonis, Book 3, sive Peri Hermeneias* (Vol. II of Delphin edition of *Opera Omnia*). London, 1825.

ARISTOTLE. *Organon,* Vol. I (Loeb Classical Library). Cambridge and London, 1938.

ARISTOTLE. *Prior and Posterior Analytics*, ed. W. D. ROSS. Oxford, 1949.

————. *Topica et Sophistica Elenchi*, ed. W. D. ROSS. Oxford, 1958.

CICERO. *Topica* and *Brutus* in *Rhetorica Vol. II* (Oxford Classical Tests). Oxford, 1903.

GELLIUS, AULUS. *Noctium Atticarum Libri XX.* Leipzig, 1903.

LAERTIUS, DIOGENES. *Lives of Eminent Philosophers.* (Loeb Classical Library). Cambridge and London, 1950.

Platonis Dialogi, 6 vols. (vol. VI contains Albinus's "Introduction to Plato's Dialogues)". Leipzig, 1892.

PLUTARCH. *Moralia*, Vol. 6, fasc. 1. Leipzig, 1954.

PROCLUS. *Commentary on the First Book of Euclid.* Leipzig, 1873.

PS.-AMMONIUS. *Commentary on Aristotle's Prior Analytics*, ed. M. WALLIES. Berlin, 1899.

SEXTUS EMPIRICUS. (Loeb Classical Library). London, 1929. Note: passages of Sextus referred to in the text as *Adv. Math.* VII or VIII occur in this edition in books entitled *Against the Logicians* I or II respectively.

SIMPLICIUS. *Commentary on Aristotle's Categories*, ed. K. KALBFLEISCH. Berlin, 1907.

VON ARNIM. *Stoicorum Veterum Fragmenta.* Leipzig, 1923, 1924.

Works on Logic or Science

BEKKER, I. *Anecdota Graeca.* Berlin, 1816.

I. M. BOCHENSKI, *Ancient Formal Logic.* Amsterdam, 1951.

————. *La Logique de Théophraste.* Fribourg, 1947.

EDELSTEIN, L. "Recent Trends in the Interpretation of Ancient Science." *Journal of the History of Ideas*, XIII, 1952.

HEATH, SIR THOMAS L. *Aristarchus of Samos.* Oxford, 1913.

KAPP, E. *Greek Foundations of Traditional Logic.* New York, 1942.

MATES, B. *Stoic Logic.* Berkeley, 1953 (Reprinted 1961).

MAU, J. "Stoische Logik." *Hermes*, vol. 85, 1957.

PRANTL, C. *Geschichte der Logik im Abendlande*, Vol. I. Graz, 1955. (Photographic reprint of Leipzig, 1855, edition.)

SCHMEKEL, A. *Die Positive Philosophie*, Vol. I. Berlin, 1938.

INDEX

Adjectives, comparative, use of, 121, 122

Aëtius, 61, 109

Affirmative of proposition, 60, 61; universal, 89, 98, 101, 129; particular, 98, 99, 101, 102, 108

Albinus, 20, 63, 79–80, 131

Alcibiades of Plato, 6, 115–16

Alexander of Aphrodiasias, 1, 2, 7, 10, 14, 21, 27, 58, 66, 67, 70, 76, 80, 93, 94, 103, 116, 117, 118, 123, 124, 129, 130, 131, 132, 133

Alternation: exclusive, 11, 12, 82, 84; non-inclusive, 82; kinds of, 84; non-exclusive, 84, 92, 113

Ammonius, 93

Antecedence, 78

Antecedent, negative; conditional with, 74, 81, 82

Apodictic syllogisms, 9, 100, 107

Apodosis and protasis, 70, 74

Apuleius, 119. *See also* Pseudo-Apuleius

Archaioi, 22

Archimedes, 105

Aristarchus, 105, 106

Aristophanes, 93

Aristotle: Galen's familiarity with, 2, 28, 85, 91, 97, 98; categories of, 6; *Prior Analytics* of, 7, 12, 25, 60, 63, 65, 71, 90, 96, 97, 98, 128, 129; metaphysics of, 8, 9; logic developed by, 10, 15; Organon of, 10, 60; Stoic view of, 11; terminology used by, 19, 65, 77, 86, 96, 97, 126; and reduction *per impossibile*, 25, 97; Posidonius familiar with, 29; *de Anima* of, 56; *Posterior Analytics* of, 56, 65, 84, 106, 122; use of hypothetical argument, 66, 68, 69, 70, 129, 131; *Topics* of, 76, 77, 96, 100; symbolism of, 91; differing from Galen, 95, 99; reduction of syllogisms, 97–98; use of categorical syllogisms, 103–4, 116. *See also* Categorical syllogisms; Categories; Peripatetics

Assumption: definition of, 59, 82, 128–29

Atomic propositions, 86

Authorship of *Institutio:* question of, 3–4

Axiom: force of, 14, 27, 29, 30, 59, 117, 124, 128; definition of, 59; role in syllogisms, 118, 123; conjoining of, 119; in relational syllogisms, 119; as premiss, 120; universal, 124, 125; arguments depending on, 126

Barbara syllogism, 97, 98, 107, 118

Baroco syllogism, 90, 97, 98, 99, 108

Bocardo syllogism, 90, 99

Bochenski, I. M., 8, 11, 67, 69

Boethius, 7, 68

Boethos, 10, 93, 131

Boethus, 15

Camestres syllogism, 98, 108

Carneades, 11

Casare syllogism, 98

Categorical propositions: classifications of, 23–24; discussed by Albinus, 79; Galen's treatment of, 88; conversion of, 89, 91, 98; definition of, 103

Categorical syllogisms: discussion of, 7, 26, 103–10; in Peripatetic logic, 9; structure of, 12; development of, 15, 19; relation to ten categories, 23–24, 26, 103, 107; relative priority of, 25; moods of figures in, 26; three figures in, 26; relationships in, 69; establishing validity of, 94; premisses of, 95, 129; common term in, 96; and relational syllogisms, 104, 116, 117, 120; and indemonstrables, 118; and mathematical reasoning, 122; axioms in, 123; Galen's use of, 124

Categories: of Aristotle, 6, 9, 60, 85, 103, 122; of Stoics, 9–10; of composition, 16, 26, 60, 108, 109–10; and categorical propositions, 23–24, 26, 103, 107; Galen's addition to, 26; and categorical syllogisms, 26, 103, 107; of quantity, 60, 108; of state,

GALEN'S *INSTITUTIO LOGICA:*
English Translation, Introduction,
and Commentary

BY JOHN SPANGLER KIEFFER

designer:	Edward D. King
typefaces:	Centaur and Plantin
compositor:	Wm. Clowes and Sons, Ltd., London
printer:	Universal Lithographers
paper:	Perkins and Squier
binder:	Moore and Co.
cover material:	Arrestox C

designer: Edward D. King
typefaces: Centaur and Plantin
compositor: Wm. Clowes and Sons, Ltd., London
printer: Universal Lithographers
paper: Perkins and Squier
binder: Moore and Co.
cover material: Arrestox C